HOW TO CHOOSE CONFIDENCE

IT'S YOUR LIFE

EMILIA OHRTMANN

IT'S YOUR LIFE

First published in 2020 by

Panoma Press Ltd
48 St Vincent Drive, St Albans, Herts, AL1 5SJ, UK
info@panomapress.com
www.panomapress.com

Book layout by Neil Coe.

978-1-784529-20-8

The right of Emilia Ohrtmann to be identified as the author of this work has been asserted in accordance with sections 77 and 78 of the Copyright, Designs and Patents Act 1988.

A CIP catalogue record for this book is available from the British Library.

This book is available online and in bookstores.

DEDICATION

For my children – Maximilian, Nicholas, Felicia and Lavinia –
who teach me and help me grow every single day.
I love you and I am forever grateful for you.

And for my mother, who planted in me a tiny seed for this
book a few years ago.

PRAISE FOR THIS BOOK

"I feel like we just had coffee and you told me your life story; and at the same time, you are so eager to encourage everyone to blossom in their own life. A very refreshing and inspiring read. Thank you."

Renske Law, branding and marketing consultant

"Enjoyed every part of your story, as I related to almost all of them. Your book made me realise that issues we think we are the only ones facing are somehow easy to handle, when seen through the eyes of someone else!"

Ghizlane Benzakour, managing partner, Table and Beyond

"An insightful book with great advice and food for thought."

Ina Kubler, HR professional

"This book dares you to dream and shows you how."

Claire Burrows, full-time mother

"A deeply personal and inspiring debut. Emilia opens up and is honest about her struggles in life, motherhood and business. Funny, witty and brilliant ideas shared, which we can start today to live our best life."

Kyla Neill, business and life coach and consultant

"This book is the guide to happiness; it has opened my eyes to many things in my life that I didn't know were affecting my thinking and decisions, and it's an easy read for the younger generation. Emilia has done a great job in writing this in such a transparent, honest way that we can all relate to it."

Jieda Sweid, founder and chief executive, Kaosys

"Emilia shows how it is completely possible to change your mindset and take charge of your thoughts and life!"

Lisa Cappuccio, founder, Luna Ink

ACKNOWLEDGEMENTS

Bringing this book to life would not have been possible without the help and support of so many people.

The biggest thank you goes to my husband and best friend, Gordon, who is always there to support me and believes in all my dreams. Without his patience and taking care of the kids on the weekends when I was writing, I would not have been able to pull this off.

Endless thanks goes to Ritchel, our nanny, for all her help with our family during the past years. I always get the question, "How do you do it all?" and the truth is, I don't. I have Ritchel to back me up, always loving and happy, always supportive. By the time this book is published, she will have gone home and will be truly missed as part of our family.

To my parents, Dagmar and Utz, for raising me to be a resilient and strong woman, I thank you. I am forever grateful that you are my parents. Your support and your unconditional love means the world to me. My sister, Johanna; her husband, Jocelyn; my brother Justus; as well as Pauline – you have always been there for me, and this is what family is truly about. Endless gratitude goes to Reinet Doig, not only for helping me so much with the editing of this book and the use of English, but also for her commitment to my book and my business, and for always being available, just a text message away.

I had no idea where or how to start writing a book until I met Mindy Gibbins-Klein, my publisher. Your great mix of kind and strict guidance, especially when doubt crept in, made this dream a reality. Thank you.

And thank you, of course, to her great team at Panoma Press for your hard work.

To my friends and colleagues who took time out to be my test readers and give me feedback – it made all the difference to the final product. Thank you, Jieda Sweid, Renske Law, Ghizlane Benzakour, Ina Kubler and Sinja Reinert, for being honest and helpful. And Janice Brieger, thanks for forgiving me years ago. Thank you, Lisa Cappuccio, Kyla Neill, Claire Burrows and Sibylle Dowding for always being there for me and for believing in me and this book.

A special thank you to Phil Bedford and the whole Asentiv community for your support.

I am very grateful for Marilou and Jerry Sweany, as well as Bina Matthews, for teaching me so much. Thank you also to Sven Maikranz and Nilam Shah and the whole MindBridge community; it would be too much to mention everyone, but so many have left a footprint in this book by listening and learning together.

Thank you to my friend Akemi Hoshi for always pushing me to run faster, and of course for your great photos.

Thank you to Farida Gilmore for allowing me to tell your story.

I do also want to mention my 'old' friends Yanin, Leslie, Cici, Jule, Katharina and Teresa – thank you so much for our long friendship and for being one of the few constants in my life.

Last, a huge thank you to my clients and my community, as well as to our Mums in Biz community and all my great interviewees, who continue to support me through reading and listening.

And of course, to YOU, the reader. You have chosen to read this book and to give some of your valuable time to my words – thank you so much. It truly means the world to me.

CONTENTS

INTRODUCTION

As I sat down and wrote this book, my story, I often had tears in my eyes. I thought about my younger self who gave away her dreams because she believed other people's opinions. The little girl who was not confident enough to believe in herself. The girl who felt judged and judged others to feel happier. The girl who thought the world was against her and so many things were going wrong. Now I think, "How could I believe that? How could I not see how much there was – there is – inside me? If I don't believe in myself, nobody else will. It was and is my life and nobody else's." I think about how much my own insecurities held me back.

I have come a long way. I have become the person I always wanted to be. And now the time has come to give back, to tell my story, so that other women like you can take away something for your own life. Some things you may know already, some may be new, some may resonate more than others, but my hope is that there will be something I can inspire you to do and to take action now.

The idea for this book came about a few years ago because I don't like to travel without my four children. I have a terrible fear of flying and over the years I have learned to deal with it, but I am afraid something will happen to me and they will have to grow up without their mum. Whenever I travel, I write them a letter, just in case. It is not a letter for them to read now, but a backup letter, if you can call it that.

One day I had to go to the hospital because I was losing a lot of blood, and I had all sorts of thoughts, "What if they won't be able to stop the bleeding? What will happen to my kids?" If you are a mum reading this, it will resonate with you more. Once you have children, life takes on a different meaning; your whole perspective changes. Your worries change and for me, I was suddenly afraid of death. So, I began writing for my children and that is how the idea of this book was born. I wanted to write down my life learnings to pass on to them. I wanted to make sure my kids would choose to live their lives, and nobody else's. I wanted to make sure they wouldn't stop fighting for their dreams and that they would stand up again and again when something went wrong. I wanted them to live happy and confident lives. Lives with confidence in themselves and others.

But this book is not only for my children to read when they are older. This book is for YOU. By writing openly about my own story, which is nothing out of the ordinary – I actually have a very blessed life, but I still struggled with many things – I want to show you that you are not alone and that it is OK. And I want to show you that there is always a way, that you have choices and that life is actually for you and not against you. I haven't figured everything out and that's OK. I am learning every day and that's good. But I know I am responsible for my life; I choose what kind of life I live. And so can you.

I never thought I was a writer. I liked it at school and was reasonably OK, but I never ever saw myself taking this any further. The writer in my family was my mum. There was somehow no space for another one. Years later I started writing a blog. I had toyed with that idea for a long time but was not sure what to write about, how much to share and how to do it really. I started blogging to support my website design business, as well as for my website to be found on Google, and I realised that I liked it. That is the simple and true answer. I started writing more on Instagram. It became more personal and people started commenting and resonating with what I had to say. People started to follow and sign up for my newsletters, wanting to read more about me and my business.

Eventually, I started a personal blog; it took me a long time to share it publicly. However, I loved it, which took me by surprise. I never realised how powerful it was to write down my thoughts and life experiences on paper – or digitally, I should say. It also became an outlet for me, once I realised that I had something to share. Maybe there is someone out there who needs to hear these words. Maybe that someone is you? Maybe there will be a time in my children's lives when they need to hear my words. Many of the things I am writing down are things I tell them now, but life will happen, other things will take over and they will forget some of it. My mother told me so many wise things, many things my grandmother had told her, and I forgot some of those lessons. I know I didn't really take them in when I was younger. I did not believe them. They did not help me. Or they just had no meaning to me at the time. But now I would love to hear them; I would have loved to read them. Now I understand my mum and my grandmother so much better.

So, when my kids reach a certain age, they may need to read these words. And my words may help you now.

With this book, I want to tell you that you will be OK. That you are perfect just the way you are. That everything is going to work out. However, it is up to you; things will happen, and you may not be able to control them, but you can control how you react to life. You have choices and you can make the right ones. They may not be my choices or other people's choices, but they need to be yours.

You make choices every single day. Small choices like what to eat for breakfast or for lunch. You choose which way to go to work, which clothes to put on, which make-up, which film to watch, which book to read – the list is endless. You also make big choices and take decisions about taking on a new job, for example, maybe even moving to a new country, getting married, having kids or buying a house. Your big decisions can have a big impact on your life or on the lives of others. And sometimes it is the small choices that you make that have the most impact on people's lives, like stopping to give a person on the street some money, which will change their day, but have almost no impact on yours.

What many people believe, and I did too for a very long time, is that so many things are not our choice, that things are determined by others, by our abilities, by the way we look, by the circumstances in our country or the country we were born in. I thought, for example, that I was not smart enough to do things, not pretty enough to ever find a boyfriend. For a long time I thought school would never end, that everything was against me, and that nobody liked me. And I thought I was shy. I did not dare say what I was thinking out of fear I could be wrong or be judged.

But who determines what is wrong? I realise now that often there is no right or wrong answer and I can say anything. If I don't know something, there are other people who don't know these things and they are glad there is someone else who admits it. Or if people laugh at something I don't know or understand, I remind myself that I know so many other things other people don't know. Maybe it's not politics I am interested in, but I know about expat life, so many cultures, design, website design, building a business, doing triathlons – the list goes on. I remind myself of these areas, and that I will never judge someone for not knowing something either. Always treat others how you want to be treated.

When it comes to opinions, they are not right or wrong either: they're just opinions. You can agree or disagree with someone, but that doesn't mean that their opinion is correct. It's still just an opinion. You choose what kind of meaning and significance you give that opinion. When I was young, I was so easily influenced. I would listen to seemingly wiser, more intelligent or just more self-confident kids and adults and think they were right. I would not do things I wanted to do, because of other people's opinions.

When I had my first therapy session with an amazing older woman – to whom I am forever grateful – she listened to my story and explained to me that I should feel sorry for this little insecure girl. And I just could not. I resented her too much. I myself had made my life so difficult. I could not feel sorry. I have always been very hard on myself – I still am. And I can be hard on other people, as well as my children. However, having kids has opened my eyes to many things. My kids have taught me so much. First, I don't need to be so hard. They have taught me to accept more and expect less, and to appreciate my younger self as well as others, to give my younger self and others a hug.

The beauty of being in my 40s is that I've had enough life experience to see many things more clearly, and now I still have enough time to live and follow my own advice. I didn't understand this – and so many other things – before, but now I do, "With age comes wisdom." When you get older, you have experienced many similar situations and feelings before, when you may have reacted the wrong way. The wonderful thing about life is that we all get second chances. You have new opportunities to make the right choice or react the way you feel is right. Becoming a mother helped me a lot. Once I became a mum, I suddenly somehow grew up. I was now responsible for another human being (or four). I am showing someone else how to live, my behaviour is being copied and I now need to make sure I am living my best life.

And this is what I want to help you with, choosing to live your life, to live a life with confidence!

CHAPTER ONE

THE TRUTH IS, IT IS YOUR LIFE

When my new friend in Dubai told me that she envied my confidence and the way I just went and did what I wanted, she didn't know what a huge compliment she had just paid me.

Whenever Gordon, my husband, asks me, "Why are you even asking me? You know what you will do anyway and don't actually want my opinion," he doesn't realise what a compliment that still is to me. He has only ever known me as confident, not listening to others and decisive.

It has not always been that way. Growing up, my belief about confidence was that you had to be outspoken, loud, maybe look different, always know the answer and basically be the perfect person. Growing up, I was everything but confident: I was very shy. And I hated myself for it. I would listen to other people's opinions;

I would judge other people and I would feel judged myself. I never raised my voice or gave my opinion. I felt that life was unfair to me and luck was not on my side. Everything seemed to be hard work. I didn't think I had any talents. I felt like this grey person, not living my own life.

What I do know is that on the inside I was suffering and few people could see that or bothered looking. And I blamed the world. I blamed my parents and other people. People who were more outgoing. People who were more daring. People who were more confident. I found many reasons to blame others. I remember being a teenager, always in a bad mood. Yes, I know this may be normal at that age, but the thing was, it was not me; it was not who I was meant to be. Even as a teenager I felt that this was not the real me.

Inside I knew that this unhappy and shy person was not who I was. Somehow, I had turned into someone I never wanted to be or thought I would be. So, I used to daydream about the woman I would be one day. I had big dreams and visions for her. However, I put all those dreams on hold because I thought it wasn't the right time for her. I thought that once I finished school, I would do it, or that once I got my first job then I would do it – I always believed there would be a better time.

Eventually I came to realise that it was my life, and nobody could tell me how to live it. It was my choice to be influenced by other people's opinions. I didn't have to listen to them. I could choose how I viewed my life, or how I let other people influence me. I had a choice to judge or feel judged; I had a choice how to show up; I had a choice how I appeared to others; and I had a choice how to feel and react. This change and realisation did not happen overnight. Unlike many other people you read about, I didn't have an epiphany or pivotal moment in life. It happened gradually, as all life lessons do.

There was a time when I found out I loved doing something and actually became good at it. Acting in the school play in 10th grade was one such moment I can recall. I don't really know how I did it, but I got one of the lead roles and totally loved it.

A little later, I left my parents' house and went to a boarding school in a country where I could hardly speak the language. This may sound simple, but remember this was before the time of mobile phones and the internet was just becoming a thing. I created my very first email address before leaving just to basically forget about it as soon as I arrived.

Moving to another country and going to boarding school was one of the best things that happened to me, for so many reasons. The first was that I could start from scratch with a clean slate. Nobody knew me – now I could be the real me and start living the life that I had always dreamed about. When I look back now, I guess I was still very shy during my time in Scotland, but it was nothing compared to how shy I was back home; it felt like two different lives.

Living in Scotland showed me that it was just me, being responsible for myself, choosing who I would be. Choosing how I'd show up every day, choosing how I would be seen, choosing how I would behave.

I took ownership of my own life. And I have done ever since.

I decided I would not wait anymore for anybody else to help me or tell me what to do. I would no longer hide high up in a tree in kindergarten waiting for the teacher to come and rescue me from the bully. I would help myself. I would speak up.

I work on my mission every single day. To live a life full of choices and confidence. I have come a very long way, and by telling my story I want to show you how you can make these choices for yourself, how you can choose to be confident. If it is possible for me, then trust me, it's possible for you.

The first step you need to take is to realise that it's your life and that you have only one shot at this thing called life. Nobody else can live it for you or can take it away from you: you are responsible. Only you can waste it and only you can make the best out of your life. If you are letting other people define your life, that is on you and nobody else. Time flies and you can't get any second back. You can't get a day back. That is why you need to make sure you're using the time you have on this beautiful place called Earth the right way. You need to use it and not waste another second.

COMPARISON

When I was growing up, I often heard sentences like, "Look how good you have it," and "Look at her; look at what she has achieved," and "Don't you want to be like her?" I felt we were being compared a lot and consequently, I did the same. I compared myself to others and vice versa; it was the way I was raised.

Somewhere along the line, I realised that this comparison game was useless. It's so useless. We are not the same. Everyone is different. We have different strengths and weaknesses. Some things come easier to others than they do to me and other things come easier to me than to them. We have different dreams and desires. Her life is not my life. My life is not hers. This is when I started questioning myself, "Am I living the life I want to live? Am I living the person I want to be?" And I realised, "This is your life; stop comparing yourself to other people."

I was always involved in some sort of sport and yet never thought of myself as a very sporty person. It didn't come easily to me. At school, we used to do these country runs, and I found them so hard.

I would look at the other girls who didn't play hockey or tennis as well as I did, but seemed to run much faster. Some of them even used to stop for a smoke in between and then carry on running as if this were the easiest thing in the world. And, of course, it bothered me. However, we are all different. I was better at other things and although being better than other people is not important to me now, I do think it's important to know your strengths. If we know our strengths, then we can work on them and use them to live our best life.

You may be thinking that you don't know what you're good at, or that there is nothing you are particularly good at, and I understand this feeling. I thought that for a long time, because I didn't feel as though I had one outstanding talent. I have come to understand now that I am good at many things, even though they may not be that obvious. You can also find your strengths. If they are not obvious to you, you may just need to dig a little deeper, ask other people, or even get help from a coach, a mentor or a therapist.

You are no doubt thinking what most people think when they hear the words 'therapist' or 'coach'. When I was growing up, my dad told me that therapists were for broken people, not for us. I still went to see a therapist when I was about 20. It was the second step to really claiming my life for myself. I can't even remember her name, and she is probably not alive anymore. I just hope she knew how much she was helping me. She set the groundwork for a life of continuing improvement and growth.

Deep down, I always knew what I was good at and what my dreams were. I also knew I would find a way to achieve them. Sometimes you need help and support from other people to make these discoveries – and that's OK. I believe that deep down you also know what you are good at, and what your dreams are. And you can find a way to achieve them.

IT IS NEVER TOO LATE

When you take ownership and control of your life, things will begin to work themselves out. You will see that your fears are not realised. You will start doing things you never thought you were capable of. You will realise that it is never too late for anything.

When I was in my late 20s, I decided to go back to university to study fashion design, something I had always dreamed of doing. I feared it was far too late to start a new career, and ended up not following my dream. How wrong I was. I am in my 40s now and have started so many new things. I'm starting new adventures every day. The amazing thing is that I am not alone – I have met people in their 50s, 60s and 70s who have started something new. I met a woman who did her first-ever triathlon when she was 50. I have read stories of women starting yoga and ballroom dancing in their 70s. I have read about a woman who took up running at 85. There are so many amazing stories out there that show us it is never too late to start something new. If they can do it, so can you!

DREAM LIST

I have a dream list. It is filled with all the things I want to do. It's a work in progress. I'm always adding new ideas and crossing off those I have achieved or are no longer that important to me. One dream at a time.

If you are someone struggling to live the life you actually want, struggling to realise your dreams, I highly recommend you sit down and do the same. Give yourself 30 minutes or more if you are trying this for the first time. Put on some nice music, turn off all the distractions and just write down everything you have always wanted to do but thought the time wasn't right. Don't think: just write. Think about all the dreams that you've had, but thought it was too late, not for you, or just not the right thing to do. Write down everything you can think of. Whatever it is that is holding you back, forget about it for these few minutes. Don't overthink. Write. DREAM.*

Now you can just leave it sitting there for the moment. Later, you can come back and put it in order of the dreams you want to accomplish this year, next year or until you reach a certain age. Or you can place your dreams in order of importance – the most important at the top and work down from there. It's up to you to decide how.

By knowing what your dreams are and having a list that you look at from time to time, you will be reminded of those dreams. You will be more likely to work on them and achieve them. I have my list because I don't want to look back at my life when I am old, and think, "I should have..."

Throughout this book, you will have the chance to come back to your list. And I would encourage you to have that list in a place where you will at least look at it. Don't let it gather dust in your drawer. Cross off your achievements, add more to your list as you grow and change, and be reminded of your dreams*.

*At the end of this book there is a page for you to dream big and write your dream list today.

BEING SELFISH

This book is called "It's Your Life" because I want you to decide. I want you to be who you truly are. I want you to be confident about your life, and it's so important for you to realise that living your life your way does not mean you are selfish.

When you are constantly being told, "You are too selfish," you begin to believe that statement even when it is not true. For a long time, this is what people in my life said: I was only thinking about myself, never about them. I was not helpful. I was not what they wanted me to be. Just as I believed I was shy because others said I was, I believed I was a selfish person for a long, long time.

I reacted in two ways: on the one side, I gave up. I didn't even try to live my dreams. On the other side, I started to look out for others, put everyone else first including their opinions. I did it in a way that was not healthy.

Although the feeling of not being selfish got better over time, it came back, big time, when I became a mother for the first time. I tried to keep up my old life as much as possible. I was convinced it would work, being a mum, working, being a good wife, cooking, being active and everything else I needed to do to make everyone happy.

Somehow the mum thing took over. Whenever I did something for myself, I felt guilty. Whenever I left my son with my husband or a babysitter – we were living in America at the time, far away from grandparents who could have helped – to do something for myself, I felt guilty. I even felt guilty when I needed surgery and Gordon had to look after Maximilian, our first son, when he was just two months old. He was constantly crying and refused to take a bottle. I knew Gordon would not be able to calm him down because Max needed to be breastfed and I felt so guilty asking for help. I felt guilty that I needed this surgery, I felt guilty for leaving Gordon with a screaming baby and I felt guilty because I was leaving Maximilian alone.

I guess it took having four kids for me to fully realise that I can't pour from an empty cup. It took having four kids to realise that my cup needs to be constantly full, overflowing in fact, in order to give so much to my family and to keep showing up for others the way I want to.

You may laugh, but I honestly never fully understood why, on an aeroplane, they say take the oxygen mask for yourself first and then help your children. I thought I would always give it to them first, until I realised I might not be able to help them if I didn't help myself first. It was such a revelation, and I feel this is so important for any mum, any woman, to understand.

Women are constantly showing up for others: their friends, their kids, their husband or partner, their employers. They often don't have the energy to show up for themselves anymore. Can you relate at all? Are you regularly showing up for yourself? Do you take time to do what you want to do? Do you work on your dreams? Are you taking the time to be active, so you stay healthy? Are you taking time to work on your hobby, be creative, do something for your soul?

I mentioned the full cup and I love this comparison. Think of a glass that only has a little bit of water inside; it is so much harder and takes so much longer to pour water from that almost empty cup for others. However, if that cup is constantly being filled with water, the water keeps on overflowing and it is easy to give to others; it happens automatically. Think of that cup as being you. If your emotional cup is full and overflowing, it is so much easier to give to others. This giving will again fill your cup as it brings so much joy to give. It becomes a wonderful cycle.

You have to make a conscious choice to keep showing up for yourself, and to do it consistently.

You have to make the choice to ensure that you are happy. That you are healthy. That you live the life you want to live.

I know how hard this can be when you feel as though you are being pulled into so many directions. When there are so many expectations of you. When your day seems to be controlled by the kids, by your work, by other people. I believe that there are times in our lives that we have more or less of these responsibilities weigh in on us. This is not an excuse to sit back and forget about ourselves. You have to make the choice to find the time for yourself. You have to choose to live the life you want – every day.

I have been an expat wife for many years. I have moved to different places because of my husband's job, and have had four kids during this time. I know what it feels like to have no control over your life. To feel as if everybody else is making decisions for you. To feel that everybody wants something from you and somehow forgot to ask you what you want. I never imagined I would be the wife following her husband's job around the world. I thought I would have my own career, make my own decisions about where I wanted to work and live. Well, that is not how it actually happened. And I'll be honest, I struggled with this decision I took years ago, and still do, often.

Maybe it's your parents or your friends; it could be your partner; and if you have kids – it's definitely your kids! And yes of course, you have to be there for them. You have to be there for your kids when they are small. However, kids grow up and they will not need you as much later in life. They will move out. They may move to another country, as I did. They will start their own families and then what? If you never lived the life you wanted to live while you had them around, what will you do when they are no longer there to fill that gap?

I have not had a 'stable' job for the past 12 years. Eek, it feels very long when I write this down. This has never held me back; I have always made sure I have something for myself. I have reinvented myself many times while moving, while pregnant, while breastfeeding, while also feeling stuck with my husband's job situation. I always know it's my choice how I deal with the situation. It is my choice how I view the situation and make the best of it. It is my life.

One of the ways I hold on to this is through my love of travel. Travel is at the top of my list of important things in my life. I have many destinations on my own dream list. However, with four kids, travelling can be not only expensive but also exhausting. Knowing what an important part exploring new countries plays in my life, I find ways to make this work for me and the kids. It may not be exactly what I would do if I didn't have kids with me. It may be more work for me, be more exhausting and it may not exactly be the way other people think travel with children should be. No matter, we have found ways to make it work for our family. It may not be your version of a holiday, but it is for us. It is possible to travel, with kids, and for everyone to have a wonderful experience.

I truly believe that you can be a mum AND a wife AND a daughter AND a daughter-in-law AND a friend AND have a career AND be active AND eat healthily. Sometimes it is not possible to do it all at the same time. Sometimes you have to do things one after the other. Sometimes you have to switch between the roles. You may have to make some compromises and things may not turn out exactly the way you thought. You have to find your way. It may take longer than you originally planned; it may be harder, but it is possible.

You could be like my friend Katharina, who started her business when she didn't have any children. She went on to grow and expand it and her family by no fewer than three children. Jenny chose to wait until her kids were 18 and at college before she started running marathons. There will never be a right time when you have kids, but there is never a wrong time either.

I believe it is possible to be many things. For me and for my life it is the way I chose to do it. Being a mum doesn't go away. Once you become a mum you will always be a mum. Whatever else you want to add to your life is your choice, just as when and how you add it is up to you. But never once believe that you are 'just' a mum and that nothing else is possible. You can be many things. You will need to ask for help; it will be hard sometimes, but it is possible, and it is worth it!

ASKING FOR HELP

Asking for help is definitely not one of my strengths. In general, I'm a person who thinks I can do it the best and the fastest. I am a controller. It's hard to admit this, but it's the truth. When I outsource work for my business and it doesn't turn out the way I want it to, I'm the first one to take over and do it myself. I haven't learned to let go and not take over. I am the same with my family. I have caught myself just doing things and not even bothering to ask my husband or the kids for help. I need to make a deliberate effort to ask them for help. And I am even worse about asking friends for help.

I get you; I know exactly what it feels like. It's this feeling that so many women have, the feeling that we have to do it all. We have to be the perfect wife, mother, friend, entrepreneur, cook, athlete, party host – and the list goes on – AND we have to do it all alone. I have come to realise that the 'doing it alone' part is not possible. If you see this on social media or know a friend that does it ALL, look a little closer: there is more to it. They may not show it, it may not be obvious, but they do have help.

I often talk about this topic in my business community: outsource, so that you can free up time for the things you are good at and you enjoy the most. I am making a conscious effort to follow my own advice and when I listen to myself, it works. For my work, it works and for my family, well let's say that we are getting better at it all the time.

Actually, you can choose, you don't have to do it all alone. Asking for help, or paying someone – such as a babysitter – for help is not a weakness. But often it is not only about asking, but also about accepting the offer of help. I'm very quick to say, "No thank you" to the offer of help. I know that so many other mums are as well. Asking for help or accepting help ensures you are also living your life. You are looking after yourself. Asking for help and accepting it means you are not totally exhausted and miserable all the time. Asking for and accepting help means you can do other things, things that bring you joy. Asking for and accepting help means you can fill up your own cup, so you are able to pour from a full cup.

Being a mum does not mean you have to be with your child 24 hours a day. Being a mum does not mean you have to give up everything else while the father gives up nothing. I have heard stories where the woman is in hospital after delivering a baby and the husband is out playing golf. I have a friend who suffers constant back pain because she is sleeping on an uncomfortable bed next to her baby while her husband gets the big bed all to himself every single night.

A child has a mother AND a father (in most cases). There should be equal responsibility. I know, it is not always possible – women are breastfeeding, for example. But you should still be able to get some time to yourself each day. To live your life. And if the help can't come from the father, it can come from grandparents, and yes, you can also get help from parents-in-law. Your mother-in-law has raised at least one son: your husband. She is perfectly capable of looking after a child for an hour. I know new mums sometimes don't believe that. I didn't. I thought I was the only one able to really look after my baby. My mother-in-law was actually a wonderful grandmother and it is a shame I can't ask her for help anymore. I would love to ask her now, and I know she would have loved to help.

An important thing to remember is that people usually like to help. They just need to be asked. Think about it: would you refuse when your friend asks you for help? Or your mum? Or your sister? Probably not. Helping other people makes us feel good about ourselves. And when you think about it that way, people like to help; it's actually a win-win situation for everyone.

Asking for help includes asking a coach or therapist for support when you don't know how to handle things or where to go next. I hope that the stigma around professional help starts to change or disappears. Even the best coaches have their own coaches. Nobody is perfect, and talking to someone neutral about certain situations can help tremendously.

STAYING HEALTHY

Something else I'm very passionate about is staying healthy. To me, this means taking the time to work out and eat well. I know it's so easy to be exhausted after a long day at work or with the kids – or both. But working out, even if it is just for 30 minutes, will make you feel better. It will make the endorphins flow. For me, it's evident with the whole family. As you can imagine, tensions can run high in a family of six, and going outside to exercise does help. Even my youngest daughter feels better when she can release her frustrations or any anger she may feel. Exercising will make you a happier person. You are the only one in charge of your own life and how long you live; you have to make sure you treat your body well.

I used to exercise because it was just what I did. I grew up with active parents and I continued that way. I married someone who loves sport. So, I realise it may be easier for me than for others. Believe me when I say, I also need to make the time. I need to get up early or stay up later. I need to make the effort to drag myself off the sofa when my kids are finally in bed to go and exercise. And I often exercise with my children. When Maximilian was a baby, I had a jogging stroller. When I was rocking my kids to sleep, I would do lunges or squats at the same time. Pre-kids, I had to make myself go for a run after work when it was already dark outside. I found ways to do it and I will share those in a later chapter. What I want to say is this: I stay active to be healthy and to feel good. I eat healthy food to help my body. I do everything I can to live the long life that I am planning on living.

Looking after yourself is not selfish. Taking the time to stay fit and healthy is not selfish. It's a choice you can make for your own life. And it is a choice you can make for your family. If you live a long and healthy life, you show your family how to do it and you can show up for your family the way you want to.

WHAT HAS HELPED ME

Something that has helped me live my life was defining my values for my life. What do I actually believe in? What is really most important to me? This knowledge helps to guide and ground me. It guides me when making decisions and how to show up for my life and for others. And it grounds me when I have destructive thoughts.

I highly recommend writing down your values. I'm not asking you to stop reading to do this now. I know at first hand that I don't always do what the author asks when I read books. I just want to read, go where the book is taking me, and not get distracted by writing something down. Nevertheless, thinking about what is important in your life helps you define what kind of life you want to live.

Start by asking yourself these kinds of questions:

- How do I see myself now? How would I describe myself?

- How would I like to see myself? How would I like to be?

- How do I want to be seen by others?

- What is it that is really important to me? For myself, but also for others. What is it that drives me? What do I live for?

- What gives me the most joy in life?

As I feel it helps to know how other people have answered these questions and what other people's values are, so that you can gain clarity in yours, let me share some of my values and some of my answers to the above questions.

For me, honesty, coupled with authenticity, is one of my highest values. Being honest with myself, other people, my children and the world – and being treated and treating others honestly – is what I strive for. Being honest is not just about telling the truth, but also about acting truthfully. It is about acting with integrity. I will always act the way I think is right, even when nobody is there to see it. I have not always done that, but I have learned and am learning every day. I want to be known as someone who can be trusted with an honest reaction and opinion, someone who stands by her word. This is also something that I teach my kids every day.

Another of my values is positivity. Being positive and happy drives me. Being surrounded by positive people not only lights me up: it truly elevates me and pushes me. I have come to a place where I find it hard to listen to negative people, even though I used to be one of them.

As I mentioned earlier, health and energy are very important to me. I admire people who seem to have a never-ending source of energy; I think I have a lot, but there are so many people out there who have my energy multiplied by thousands. Which is something I am striving towards.

I never want to stop growing, developing and learning. I'm not perfect. There are many areas in my life that I work towards improving every single day by taking tiny steps. As you may guess, I find people who are into self-development fascinating and I have been reading and trying out different things for many years now. I want to live a life that is worth emulating and to do that I need to become better at it, all the time.

Another of my values is giving. I want to give back to others, I was blessed with a fortunate life and I feel there is enough to share. Giving can come in many forms. Money is just one form; being active in a community, sharing knowledge and being there for someone else are also forms of giving.

Family. My family is the most important part of my life. They come first and I make sure I am really there for them. There are times when I am too busy with something else and if my family is suffering for it, I take a step back and remind myself what is more important right now. It's always my family.

Although I have not dived deep into values, I hope you get an idea of how I go about defining my values and that it has given you a starting point for defining your own values for your life.

Oh, and values don't have to be set in stone. They can change and develop. Often, they adapt when life changes. Big changes may include getting married or having children, starting a new, big job or losing a loved one.

What I find is that my values really help me to stay connected to the life I want to live. They bring joy to me and to others. And they help me to make decisions that feel right. When I am not sure how to react, what to do or what to think, I remind myself of my values and that always helps.

While writing this book, the whole world is affected by the Covid-19 virus. Even though this is not the topic of my book, my values help me stay grounded during this difficult and ever-changing situation. Many drastic measures are being taken in Dubai, where I currently live, to protect everyone. Developments around the world are crushing. In addition, I have days where I'm frustrated about not being able to work because my kids are home, and we are trying our best with home schooling and keeping our kids motivated.

The point is that I remind myself constantly that I want to stay positive. I want to show my kids that I am positive and how to stay positive in challenging times. Unfortunately, being impatient is something that comes very naturally to me. It's something I'm not proud of. I am constantly being tested on what it means to grow and be better every day. And to show my kids that there is a different way from losing it completely when something doesn't go their way.

So, if you want, take a pen and paper, set yourself a timer for about 30 minutes and just write your values down. Stick them somewhere you can see them every day and take it from there. You can adapt and change them as your life develops.

Always remember that you are living YOUR life. Nobody else's. Remember that you have only one go at life and that it ends at some point. You are not selfish when you want to make the best of your life. Only you know your dream for your life, so you need to make sure you are living for your dream.

WHAT I HAVE LEARNED IS THAT I ALWAYS HAVE A CHOICE FOR EVERYTHING IN LIFE:

1. I have the choice to live my life. It is nobody else's responsibility or choice.

2. I have the choice to stay active and healthy.

3. I have the choice to ask for help and accept help.

4. I have the choice not to compare myself, but live my own dream.

5. I have the choice to live in the now.

CHAPTER TWO

THE LESS JUDGMENTAL YOU ARE, THE MORE CONFIDENT YOU BECOME

Unhappy people criticise; happy people praise. Have you heard this saying before? I don't know where I heard it or if it's a quote I need to credit to a specific person. I have come to realise that it's true, and it is a shame I had not heard it earlier in my life. Maybe I did, but I suppose it did not really sink in then.

Judging – this is a topic I feel so strongly about. And although I don't like generalisations, judging is something everyone is guilty of at some point. My feelings about judging are so strong that it deserves a chapter of its own. It needs to be addressed so we can get it out of the way and move on. Judging is also a choice you make. And although you may want to achieve exactly that, it does not make you happy. Judging does not make you confident. Being less judgmental comes first. As you judge less, your confidence will increase. This happens automatically.

But let me start by admitting, even though it is hard, that I have been a very judgmental person. I judged left, right and centre. I was judging my friends; I was judging strangers; and of course I was judging myself. I judged because I was not confident, I was not happy with myself, so I found flaws in others and myself. It made me feel better, especially when someone else agreed. But this feeling never lasted long. Sometimes a minute, sometimes a little longer. In the back of my mind, I knew it was wrong. And I have said many things I am not proud of.

When I was younger, I was part of a group of girls who would gossip about other girls behind their backs. I gossiped about my friends with other mutual friends. I felt stronger when I was not alone. Stronger in the joint forces against someone else. Her different looks, her behaviour, her voice or anything else a 14-year-old girl can make spiteful comments about. Rather than saying the right thing, I kept quiet – which is the same thing in my eyes now. I followed others or even took the lead in gossiping, sniping and talking behind someone else's back. Whatever you may call it – judging, gossiping, sniping – it's bad. I wanted to be part of a group. I wanted to belong and not be the person they were talking about. So, I talked about others. I wanted to hide my own insecurities. It's a very common behaviour, I know, but that is not an excuse. I have seen kids and adults who are not like that and, believe me, they earn my utmost respect. I honestly think it is the part of my life I am least proud of.

Not judging, not being judgmental, is another important value that I teach my kids all the time. Some days I succeed, some days not. My hope is that they will hear my voice and essentially their own voice in their head and stand up for others who are being judged or excluded, rather than follow the crowd.

The surprising fact is that we often judge and talk bad about things that we are not good at or that we feel insecure about in ourselves. It is a protective measure. When I hear my son making fun of his younger sister because she can't do something that is 'so easy' I cringe inside. I try to explain to him what he is doing; I ask him how he would feel if other people said that about him. Sometimes it has an immediate effect; sometimes it doesn't. However, I am confident that in the long run, they will know how to behave with integrity. I get it though; all he is trying to do is to distract from his own inability to do something kids at his age are expected to be able to do.

I was the same. I judged other people's appearance and looks and at the same time I felt insecure about my own body, about my appearance and even my behaviour. I was insecure in general, so what better way to distract from that by talking about others and their faults?

Something else that I feel has contributed very much to my behaviour is that I grew up in a family that talked a lot about other people. Believe me when I say that I have a hard time writing this. It feels as if I am judging my parents or speaking ill of them. On the other hand, I know how much our environment influences us. When I grew up it was normal that we, as kids, were asked our opinion of someone we had just met, "So, what did you think of her?" I wanted to answer my parents, so it got me thinking about that person. I would look for something that I may not have necessarily noticed at first. Things that may not have been important at all. I remember driving in the car, and we would comment on the body shape and appearance of people walking by. About someone being too fat or someone having a big tattoo or someone wearing no shirt. We judged from afar people we did not know at all. I honestly still wonder why we did that and what we got out of it.

JUDGMENT IS THE WORST ENEMY OF HAPPINESS

This is a statement to think about (it is one of many that I have stuck up on my wall): Judgment is the worst enemy of happiness.

Why do people think it will make them feel good when they talk about someone else behind their back?

I don't mean the kind of positive talk between people when discussing someone else's new job or move to another country or something that we admire or find exciting. It would be even nicer if we said that to the person directly, but I know that is not always possible. I also know that complete non-judgmental behaviour is almost impossible. I'm referring to that mean talk, when what is being said is not nice in any way. Even in the slightest. I mean when an opinion is voiced that is not necessary or does not contribute to anybody's lives. I know exactly when I'm behaving in a way that I actually don't want to, and it is not contributing to anybody's happiness. Especially not my own.

I remember once talking to a dad from my kids' school and he started saying horrible things about the teacher and how unhappy he was with the school. Although I could see where he was coming from, I was shocked by the way he described some people at the school as useless and compared them to pub-drinking Englishmen who finally felt powerful because their position gave them what they had never had before. I asked whether he had spoken to the teacher and the school, and his answer was that nobody listens anyway and there is no point. Instead he talked to me about the teacher and all the mistakes the school was making. And yes, I wondered what difference that would make. Did it make him feel better? Did this help his kids, who are essentially not getting the education he wished for? Should it discourage or encourage me?

I don't believe that. I decided that I would either do something about it or keep quiet. And in this case, I am constantly trying to do my part in helping the school to be a better school by speaking up and being engaged.

What did any of us – the father, the teacher, even I – gain from him speaking in this way? Nobody should talk about someone else this way. Especially not in front of kids. And it makes me wonder, why do grown-ups still make the same mistakes they made when they were young?

I have decided that I will not say things about others behind their back just because I feel like it in that situation. Especially when nothing will come of it and I will just forget about it anyway. I know I don't always succeed, but I catch myself doing it now. And I usually realise why I am doing it. In general, if someone or something affects me, I will talk directly to that person or I will see what I can do about it. Otherwise, I accept the person or situation as they are and do not let it affect me. Yes, it does take courage to speak up. Confronting people about a behaviour that I believe adversely affects me or my family is not easy. But it does make me feel better, and the other person is better off once it is said and done.

The problem with judging is that it does the opposite of what we think it will. Instead of making you feel better, it makes you feel worse in the long run or, in the case of the dad at school, most likely just makes him feel more miserable the longer his kids go to the school and the problem with the teacher continues. Think about it: when last did you wish someone else ill? Did it make you feel any better? Especially when it happened? My guess is not. On the contrary, you most probably felt guilty and tried to hide that feeling. You lied about it to yourself to make yourself feel better again.

Do you see how we are getting back to our values? It is my value to act honestly, and with integrity. For me, that means not talking about other people behind their backs. It is also my intention to share my positive comments with that person directly, so that we both feel happier.

Judging is something that we don't often really see or realise that we are doing. As I said, I judged all the time as a teenager. I knew what I was doing. I even knew that it was coming from my own insecurities. Later on, however, I still judged, often without realising. I judged a girl at the office for wearing a very short skirt or showing too much cleavage. I judged a person at the supermarket checkout for taking so long. I judged someone else for having a large tattoo that I did not like, for having a nose ring, for talking too loud, for listening to music too loud or for voicing an opinion that I didn't agree with. There are so many examples of it being so easy to be judgmental. I didn't realise it was judging. How could I decide what was the right appearance or the right tone of voice, and why should I know better? I didn't know their situation or their special circumstances. Honestly, often it just comes down to having different tastes.

Once I came to this realisation, I decided to make some changes. I would try to understand everyone else. I would try and understand their point of view, but somehow I ended up judging my own feelings. I excused someone for cutting me off in traffic and then still felt bad about missing my turn. I was making excuses for their behaviour, but at the same time I thought it was unfair to me. Eventually I learned to choose to be calm on the inside and neither judge nor feel bad about situations. It all came back to making the choice to be confident, confident in myself and my beliefs.

REALISING WHAT I DID WAS THE FIRST STEP

I met my friend Anna early on at university and we used to take the train together to and from classes. Anna was also friends with another girl called Julia whom I didn't know very well. At uni, they were always together. One day, Anna had a terrible car accident and was in hospital for a long time. During that time, my close friend Cat left, and Julia and I became friends. We spent a lot of time together and I don't remember how it happened exactly, but Julia somehow convinced me that the absent Anna should not be our friend anymore. I think Anna realised what was happening, while in hospital, but she could not really do much about it. When she came back, she was suddenly the real outsider. It was a horrible time for her. And it lasted a few months. We were the meanest women – I really can't say girls anymore – and I have no idea how it really happened or why I participated. I feel inclined to write that I got dragged into this behaviour. However, that is not true; at the end of the day, it was my choice and nobody else's fault, even if I was just tagging along. All I know is that there came a time when I realised what I had done, and I made the choice to never let this happen again.

Today Anna and I are still close friends; we all apologised, and she forgave us. Whenever I think back about this, it brings tears to my eyes. Tears of shame, but more importantly tears that embody her pain. Did my behaviour make me feel better? No. Not in the slightest. Temporarily, maybe, because I had a friend just for myself, although I don't know if that was really the reason. What I do know is that my own behaviour still makes me feel sick 20 years later.

By telling this story I want to spread awareness. I don't want this to happen to anyone. These days I would rather exclude myself than exclude someone else. I also want to show that it is possible to fail, to admit it, to apologise and make a friendship even better.

I made four choices back then: first, not to judge nor to gossip; second, not to exclude anyone; third, if I didn't like to be around a person I would just keep my distance and stay away; that's it. And the last choice was that friendships of three are possible.

I won't say that I succeed all the time, but by realising what I have done, I have become aware and every day is a new chance to behave according to my choices.

JUDGING MUMS

Let's talk about judging mums. I'm sure you have experienced this as well: women without children judging mothers and mothers judging other mothers about how to raise kids. Oh my God, there is so much judging going on. And I have been guilty of this as well. Before I had kids, I would be on a plane thinking, "Why can't the mum two rows in front of me keep her child quiet? Why on earth does the dad not say anything when their child is lying on the floor screaming at the supermarket checkout? Why does that child constantly interrupt a conversation and the mother doesn't say anything? Why does that child always have a runny nose and the mum doesn't wipe it clean?"

I am sure most of us are guilty of those or similar thoughts and you know what I am talking about. Here's the thing: WHO are we to judge? What right do we have? How do I know the situation of that child and the mum on the plane? Maybe they are both just exhausted? How can I judge the dad for letting his child scream on the floor? I don't know their reasons, their family circumstances. Maybe he just had a horrible day at work and can't deal with another argument?

I have to admit that I had a lot of these thoughts *before* I became a mum myself. Now I'm not so quick to think anything like that anymore. I have been the mother on the plane with a screaming child or a child that spills orange juice over someone else's white trousers. I have been the mum in the supermarket with a child throwing a tantrum on the floor; I have been in a lot more and a lot worse. There was always a reason, I had tried my best, I had tried different ways and still I know that I or the kids were behaving in a way that people who don't know can easily judge. Believe me, a screaming child on the plane, in a supermarket, at school drop-off or anywhere else for that matter is worse for the parents themselves. When I travel alone these days, I don't even hear other kids anymore. I tune them out.

When we went on a family holiday to Ethiopia, we landed there in the middle of the night. At the same time, there was another plane that had just landed from Germany and I noticed a dad alone with his two sons in the row at customs. He was not very patient with his sons, who needed to go to the toilet but obviously didn't want to go alone. He did not want to leave his place in the queue and told them off for needing to go so often and needing him as well. It would have been very easy to judge him for the way he treated his kids. However, the wait in the queue took forever, all the kids were extremely tired, and the parents were also exhausted. In addition, his younger son seemed to have had some stomach problems during the flight, and even though I did not like the way the dad behaved, having been in similar situations I could feel for him. I did not judge him; instead I tried to help.

Another situation that comes to mind, and this was much harder to deal with and not judge, happened at a barbecue with our whole family. As we were leaving, walking towards the car, a boy who was about 8 years old came running up to Maximilian, who was about the same age, and just kicked him hard in his stomach. It was totally out of the blue and without any reason. They did not know each other and had not played together. Gordon was furious and went to the mum to tell her what had happened and to take care of her son better; she didn't say anything. There have only been a few times when I have seen Gordon so angry. And I admit, we judged the mum for raising a son who would behave like that and we judged her for her totally unfazed reaction. Although I do not agree with that kind of behaviour, I don't know the situation of that particular family. The son could be a special needs child, the mum could be a single mum who is overwhelmed by raising her kids alone. I don't know and I have not seen them since, but we no longer judge her and instead we use this example to talk to our kids about such behaviour and how to react if something like that were to happen to them again.

THE UNIVERSE IS TAKING CARE OF JUDGING

I believe that the universe or God or karma (call it what you want) has a way of making you pay for actions such as judging and gossiping. I don't know when and I don't know how, but I will have to deal with the consequences at some point.

I have seen this karmic payback happen (also to myself) when friends try to exclude one another, only to be the ones left out at the end.

When I lived in London, I knew a group of four friends who used to do everything together. They would plan holidays and short trips together, spend time over the weekend together – I'm sure you know the scene.

As happens in this transit city, Emily moved away, and the friends saw each other a lot less often as a group. Alexandra was never as fond of Emily as the other three were, and after a very heated argument one day they stopped talking to each other.

Alexandra started excluding Emily from gatherings and then from the plans the friends were making for the next group holiday. Alexandra assumed that everyone had the same feelings about Emily. It appeared to her that she was succeeding. What she did not realise was that the three friends had met up for coffee and it was just like old times. Emily told them how much she missed her old hometown, her friends and the trips they used to take. So, they told her about their next planned trip and invited her to come along. Alexandra was devastated; she felt she really could not spend time with Emily anymore and decided not to join their planned holiday. Now she obviously felt excluded and upset. Instead of making things right with Emily or just realising that in the grand scheme of things their argument was not as important, she was now the one being left out.

I have experienced a similar situation, when I demanded absolute loyalty from mutual friends after an argument with another in the group. I felt that if they were not loyal to me, they were not my real friends. It was just not true though. Just because I didn't choose to be friends with someone, it didn't mean that other people couldn't be friends with them. It is up to me, nobody else, how I deal with it.

SOCIAL MEDIA

Something that wasn't around when I was a teenager or even in my early 20s, and which makes judging so much easier, is social media and the internet in general. I'm a member of a few Facebook expat and mums' groups, and what I sometimes read in there makes me shudder. The same is true when I, very rarely, read comments on articles that have been published by magazines online. The hateful comments are often overwhelming. I wonder if people have nothing better to do with their lives than slamming other people on the internet. I get that it is easy to judge from behind a computer, often behind some sort of pseudonym. What do people think they get out of it? If it makes them feel better, it can't be for long, and it surely doesn't make them happy or confident.

I would like to make everyone aware about thinking before you post. Even if you believe you have more knowledge about the topic. In one of my groups, a friend of mine posted a photo of some flowers she had picked in the woods and wished everyone a happy day. It was a super nice post. And still there were people who lectured her to not pick those flowers. A heated discussion arose about whether or not you should pick flowers and the intent of her post; the happiness that she wanted to spread was lost. Please think before you comment. What will you gain from commenting? How might the person you are writing this to feel after your comment? Is it a helpful comment? Will you feel better? At whose expense? Is it necessary to engage on social media like that?

I have been an expat for more than 15 years. I love social media and I use it quite a lot. It's a great way for me to stay in contact with friends I have met around the world. It is a great way to share a little bit from my life and a great way to meet new people. I met a very good friend of mine, Lisa, through a Facebook group, and so far we have only ever met online. As well as being great for staying in contact and meeting new people, social media plays a part in marketing my business and reaching potential customers all over the world.

I take advantage of and really enjoy the fact that we can read newspapers online and keep up with what is happening in other parts of the world while being far away. However, I personally want to use the internet to spread positivity, love, peace and confidence.

That is what I have chosen. For myself, for my family and the world. Every time someone writes a short sentence online, it may stay there forever. Somewhere in the depths of the algorithms it can be found even years and years later.

Considering this, I make a choice before I post, share, answer or comment. Is that really something I want to share with the internet? Is that how I want to show up? I think about my values. Mine is positivity. If I write a comment that is not positive, does that align with what I have decided to stand for in this world?

TRAVELLING

Being an expat, combined with my love of travelling, has taught me another lesson that I would like to share with you. It's an experience that my kids have every day and they don't realise it; I am so grateful for it. You can't judge people according to their race, appearance, skin colour, the way they speak or even the way they greet you. I have met so many different people from around the world in many different situations. People dress differently, eat different things, have different eye or hair colour, speak English with a different accent, greet you with a hug, handshake, nothing at all or even with their shoulder (a greeting style we discovered on our travels to Ethiopia). I have met people who are chief executives of big companies, but you would never guess it from looking at them. You just can't know about people from their appearance and can't judge anybody.

We have lived in Dubai for more than eight years, and the best part of living here and having my kids grow up here is that there are people from all nationalities living together. Every family is different. We have Indian, South African, English, Spanish, Danish, Irish, Portuguese, Pakistani, Dutch, Lebanese and French neighbours, and so many people from other countries living around us. Our kids go to the same school, they play the same games, they trade the same Pokémon cards, they listen to the same music, they play the same sports together and there are no differences. And they don't notice any differences.

It helps that everyone wears a school uniform and the only way they can really make a fashion statement is with their shoes (which still must be black) and their backpacks. After school, they all put on different clothes and there is no real theme going on as there was when I was growing up in Germany, or what I still see there. Here it seems that it just doesn't matter. The parents are so different: they wear totally different clothes; some wear the local or the Indian national dress and there is just no common trend. I know the kids don't care about the clothes someone else wears. They care about common interests. That is what makes it so great to live in the UAE. I wish more people around the world were like that. Time will tell what impact this will have on my kids, but from what I can see now is that they grow up a lot less judgmental towards people from other nationalities than I ever was.

When I was growing up, I was taught that you have to put both hands on the table while eating. Never have one hand below the table. When I moved to Scotland, I suddenly saw everyone eating with one hand under the table. Initially, I was shocked. I thought they had no manners, until I spoke to someone about it and learned about all the different table rules and words in the UK versus Germany. So, what is the right way? There is no right or wrong way. I keep telling my kids to not eat their food with their hands, but in a lot of countries that is normal, and people always eat with their hands. When we travel and I start eating with my hands, because it's just the way it is done in that part of the world, my kids are so happy and think it is the best part of being away from home. These are just small examples of how people are raised differently and should not be judged because of it.

As a kid, I judged other kids because they were wearing different clothes. And I felt judged. This is still an issue in so many parts of the world, unfortunately. The pressure that is placed on some kids is huge. They want to fit in, they want to belong. I feel for these kids. Having experienced this myself I know how left out and lonely it can make you feel.

FEELING JUDGED

I felt judged very often and I still feel like that now, sometimes. Especially from people I care about. Sometimes I know they are judging because they tell me; sometimes it's a subtle feeling – you know this particular look or comment you get. It's normal, it is a normal human feeling and I am sure most of us feel it. Some more so, some less.

However, the more confident you are in your own values, in your way of life, the less you will feel judged. The less you judge other people, the less you will feel judged. When you stop judging, your awareness will turn elsewhere. It turns towards happiness and what is really important. Your life, your dreams and aspirations. What you think, decide and do. And it is the small things in life that bring happiness.

If I still feel judged, I make myself look at the situation from the outside, I change perspective and mostly realise that my feeling does not make sense. But more on that later in the book. Once I have analysed the feeling and I'm sure I am being judged, I use a method that a coach taught me, and which I often fall back on. I have learned to turn the feeling of being judged into compassion. I put myself in the other person's shoes and think why they could possibly think that way about me. What are their reasons and motives? And then I feel sorry for them for having those feelings, for being so unhappy or insecure in themselves that they have to judge someone else. I start feeling compassion for them and I choose to look for the good in the other person. It works for me. Sometimes it's easier, sometimes it's harder. And usually it depends how important that other person is to me.

Judging is something that will never go away completely. My main aim with this chapter is to raise awareness. I want you to catch yourself when you judge. Be aware and be better next time.

WHAT I LEARNED: JUDGMENT IS A CHOICE:

1. When I decided not to judge anymore, I became a happier and more confident person.

2. When I decided not to judge anymore, I felt less judged myself.

3. I realised that happy people praise, unhappy people judge.

4. The more confident I am about myself and my values, the less I judge and the less I feel judged.

5. I choose to look for the good in other people. I choose compassion for someone who feels the need to judge.

CHAPTER THREE

YOU HAVE TO LET GO OF THE PAST

Once upon a time, there was a man who was wandering through the forest and he was full of fears and bad feelings. He was thinking of his past and all the things that had gone wrong, that had been unfair, and how people had treated him badly. "I just don't want to feel this way anymore," he thought to himself.

Deeper into the forest, he saw the wise sage of the forest standing by a tree. The sage had his arms wrapped around the tree. "Oh great sage," said the man, "can you help me? I've been plagued with great fear and anger about my past for a long time and I just can't stand it anymore. Can you give me the knowledge to get rid of my fear and anger?"

"I can certainly help you," said the sage, "but first I have to wait until this tree lets go of me."

"But sir," said the man, "the tree isn't holding you; you are holding on to it!"

The sage smiled. "That is my lesson," he said as he let go of the tree and disappeared into the forest.

My NLP course teacher, Marilou Sweaney, told a slightly different version of this story and I really wanted to include it in this chapter of the book. It sums up everything I want to say here. If we want to be free, we need to decide to let go.

WHERE YOU COME FROM

Parents have a profound influence on their children. There are numerous studies about cognitive, emotional and even physical development during different ages of a child. While I don't want to go into depth here, I do need to state how crucial a healthy environment is for the development of children. Not only for their physical development, but also for their emotional development. Although every child is born unique, they are born with a clean sheet, which the world starts writing on from day one. But because each child is unique, they will react to similar situations in different ways. Every child, in some way or another, learns and adapts through what they experience, what they see and how they are raised. Certain events will stand out for some kids and not for others. You may remember an event from your childhood forever, while your family has totally forgotten about it. That event stands out for a reason you may not even be aware of.

We grow up with a set of values that our parents have passed on to us. Beliefs we were told were right or wrong. Sometimes it's done intentionally, and sometimes just by living and behaving a certain way.

Something that resonated with me was what I read in *The Code of The Extraordinary Mind* by Vishen Lakhiani is that apart from our immediate family, the surroundings, the religion, the values and rules of the country, city and the culture we grow up in has a huge impact on us. All of this is somewhat ingrained in us from an early age. From when we are born. We are told how to behave, how to eat, how to pray, how to meet people, how to judge, what and how to study, what kind of job is the right one – and the list goes on. We believe and trust in these things that are given to us and the way we should live.

However, this may not necessarily be the right way for you as an individual.

You need to figure out the right way for yourself. You need to look beyond what you know and have learned, to live your dream life.

LABELLING

I used to believe many things I was told while growing up and adapted my behaviour to those beliefs. The one that stuck the most was the label that I was shy. I believed it. And it transformed into thinking that I was not only shy, but also insecure. That again developed into a feeling of being stupid. When I was totally being myself, I was not shy or insecure (or stupid for that matter). But when I did not feel safe; the voices in my head replayed those beliefs passed on over many years and became so overpowering that I started behaving the way I felt was expected of me.

Every year, in my school reports it said, "She needs to participate more during class time." I knew it; I didn't need to be told every year, over and over again. When I wasn't behaving as expected and received great praise for it, I knew that the person who praised me meant well and wanted to encourage me. However, it created the opposite effect. I felt as if I was being told that this was unusual behaviour for me. It took me years to understand my own paradoxical thinking, and I know it was almost impossible for other people who only meant well to have known. This experience has made me very careful when I talk to my kids about their potential pain points.

In my family, we were labelled in terms of what you were or how you behaved. It was very hard to get rid of those labels. We all had a behaviour or talent that kind of stuck with us: one of us was the sporty one; one was the shy one; one was the helpful one; one was the techie person; one the artsy one; and one was the person with an aptitude for languages, while the other had a love for books. Once your label place was taken, it could not be occupied by another one. Sometimes one of us did something – such as having car troubles a few times – and the label was there. She can't drive. And it was, and is, to this day almost impossible to get rid of it.

I was labelled as the unhelpful one. My sister was the helpful one. As the label of the helpful person was already taken, I knew I had no chance of getting it. Therefore, I didn't need to try anymore. To this day, my family believe that I am not helpful. The funny thing is that other people think completely differently. Often, I am the person who forgets about herself and is thinking of others first. I am the one who helps all the time.

It was made worse for me once other people, often without any bad intention, confirmed the label. Kids laugh at other kids without any real bad intention; often they are just glad they are not being called out themselves. This was the breaking point for me. For example, I thought I was stupid because I could not remember the capital cities of our German states, while my siblings thought it was so easy. Did they laugh? I'm not sure anymore; they didn't have to. Any doubt in my mind about this label being wrong was instantly erased and I knew it was now glued to me. "She just does not know anything; she is stupid." Even though in this case it was only I who really thought that.

You can have other people attach labels to you. You can attach labels to yourself. Either way, it is up to you to accept them.

It took me many years – plus therapy, coaching, seminars, yoga, meditation, and support from my husband and friends – to get rid of these labels in my head. I have talked to so many women who have gone through similar feelings. It does take some time. It is normal.

Now that I have kids, this is something I have sworn to myself I will never, ever do to them. When I have thoughts like that, I immediately dismiss them. I know I can't treat every child totally the same. I know my children are all different and have different talents and likes, but I am not going to tell my kids what they are, who they are or who they should be. I want them to find out for themselves and I will support them in this process. Time will tell whether it is working. Maybe my kids still feel labelled in some sort of way. But my hope is that they will grow up and read this book and realise, "Yes, that is something she didn't do and yes, that is something I won't do to my kids."

Something else I came to realise is that adults often want to understand the 'why'. For example, I think about why I like someone more than others. I've caught myself asking my children why they didn't want to play with someone I had arranged a playdate with because I was friends with the mum and we had kids the same age, so it appeared to be a natural fit. Even when my kids were little, they refused to play with some kids. They don't know why they don't like someone as much as someone else. They can't put it into words. And you know what, that's OK. I ask myself why I pushed them to tell me why they didn't want to play with that kid? Why did I not just accept it? There does not need to be a reason, an explanation. There does not need to be a label for everything, for everyone.

There are things I could blame my parents for. And I have. I worked through many issues related to them, some of which I am still working on. There have been a lot of bad feelings from my side. I thought I had to really understand my past and everything that happened. However, there came a point when I realised that it was my life; I can recognise the past, I can accept, forgive and then let go to live in the now. I can choose.

ACCEPTANCE

What has helped me is to accept? To accept people as who they are. To accept their behaviour and then choose how I react to it. It has helped me to believe that everyone does things with the best intentions. Now, I know that my parents, my teachers and the people in my environment were doing the best job they could with the tools they had and still do. Nobody means to be hurtful. Things happen, everyone was raised a certain way and we are all different. If a person tells me something and then tells you the same thing in the exact same way, we will still perceive it differently. Their words are framed by our beliefs and experiences, which affects the way we understand what is being said. This is human nature. So, I learned, and to be honest, I am still learning every day not to be affected by the things that are not helping me. My time on this Earth is limited and I want to make the best of it, without having the past hang over me.

You may have experienced people saying things to you that you didn't like, treating you badly, being a bad influence. Maybe it was even your parents. If you choose to accept and to believe that they did what they did with the best of intention and that they may not have known any better, it will help you to be free. Your parents brought you into this beautiful place called Earth; they gave you life. And now it is up to you to make the best of it. To live your best life. And nobody else's.

FORGIVING

I made a choice. I will not hold anyone responsible for something they have done 'to me'. It is so easy to blame others. But essentially by doing that we are moving our attention to them instead of focusing on ourselves. They might not have known any better either or they don't even know or realise what they have done. So it is up to me to focus on myself and become better. The first step to do this is to forgive. To forgive the other person and to forgive yourself.

I love my family, no matter what. However, I have struggled a lot because of the way I was treated when growing up. And for a long time I blamed my parents. Once I decided this is not who I want to be and chose to forgive I felt a huge relief. I forgave my parents for the things I thought they had done wrong. I forgave my teachers – I had a few teachers who I did not like at all and I blamed for being unfair to me. And I forgave other people who I thought had treated me unfairly.

I know it is not easy, but let me tell you it is so worth it in order to feel free. I admit I still sometimes fall into the trap of blaming, but now I can catch myself early on and honestly I feel so much better once I stop blaming someone else, forgive and just see how I can make the situation better.

I have also forgiven myself. It took years. I was so angry with myself for being shy, for behaving over and over in a way I didn't want to.

I was upset that I did not speak up when I wanted to. I was told I needed to feel sorry for that little girl – my younger self – and I just couldn't. As I write this book, I am at peace with my past and my past self. I have felt sorry for the little girl inside me; I have hugged her and am looking after her. And I have forgiven myself. I also know I wouldn't be who I am now without having experienced my past.

That is another life lesson I want to pass on to my kids. Things may be hard sometimes, but things happen for a reason. There will be a positive outcome of some sort. And we need to let go of the hard feelings for the good ones to come.

LETTING GO AND FEELING GRATEFUL

Once I went through these steps, I was able to let go. To let go of the things that could affect my behaviour today in a way I don't want them to. I have made the choice that I will concentrate on the positive instead of the negative. It is human nature to think about the problems and the negatives – you just need to open the newspaper to see that people are obviously more interested in the bad stories than in the positive ones. What I decided to do is to learn from the negative, the negative in my past, my behaviour and other people's behaviour.

We tend to remember the highs and the lows in our lives more easily because of the way they make us feel. People remember feelings rather than actual words or behaviours. Think about the things you remember from the past: they are most likely things that were amazing and made you feel good, or things that went very wrong and perhaps made you feel really small, angry or hateful. The emotions stick with you. And what I learned about the negative feelings is that our brain makes a choice either to forget about them and bury them or to remember them as a form of protection, so it doesn't happen again, as a warning. If anything happens that makes us feel similar, we retreat into our protective behaviour. This behaviour can be anger or sadness, or running away, or staying quiet, as I did.

I decided to choose to remember all the positives in the past. I think back to a memory that made me feel good. Memories such as when I was on a holiday with my whole family; when I was sailing with my dad; or when I went on a backpacking trip with my sister. I have a lot of positive memories with my friends, and even of good times at school. I have come to a place where I remember and see something positive in everyone, even in the people I used to dislike. I have chosen to look for the good in other people.

I am sure that even for people who experienced a horrible childhood there must be a few positive moments they can remember and focus on – even something as simple as a smile. Maybe you just have to dig harder. Choosing to think of the positive things will give you power and good vibes. It will help you to let go of negative feelings that are damaging you.

LEARNING FROM THE PAST

I decided to learn from my past. I have taken everything I need, and created a roadmap of how I want to live now and how I want to raise my kids. Apart from that, I have put my past to rest and I will leave it there.

I once saw a therapist because I needed help with some questions that I had about raising my kids. I had a lot of doubts about whether I was doing the right things, or whether I had done too many harmful things. The best advice I took away from that session was that the fact that I am taking the time to reflect, that I am aware of my behaviour and that I am willing to learn, makes me so much more aware than most parents. That has helped me immensely and I often think about that advice, not only in terms of raising my kids but in general. Being aware of our own behaviour is the first step.

I learned that I am not alone, and that action is better than no action. Making mistakes is normal, but learning from them to become a better person and to improve is not. So, don't stop; everyone makes mistakes. It is human. Make sure you learn from your mistakes – this is essential. It is called growth. There is another day: it's called tomorrow, and you can be a little bit better every day. You can grow every day.

Apart from not labelling my kids, I have also learned to be very careful with the use of the world ALWAYS.

Just because it seems like it, things don't *always* happen; people don't always behave a certain way all the time. It's just not true. I may have been shyer than others; I may have been lazy sometimes. But I wasn't always shy or lazy, and neither are you. You are not always too loud, too tired, too grumpy, too strict, too big, too small, too soft, too nice or anything else that you keep telling yourself. It is not always. It is sometimes.

LIVING IN THE NOW

I have come to realise that my past no longer has control over me. Even my immediate past. Things have happened and they are over. I can't change them anymore. But I can choose to move on and live in the now.

This is not only for things that have happened to me, or the people who have caused them. This is just as true about things I have done or said. Even in the more recent past. I haven't always treated

Gordon the way I wanted to, nor my kids. I have been impatient, and there have been times when I screamed at my kids in a way that I promised myself I would never ever do again. My own behaviour has sometimes been my worst nightmare. I know I was using the coping mechanism of my father, what I had learned growing up. For a long time, I beat myself up about behaving the same way. However I learned to stop, that the anger towards myself did not help. I had to learn from my behaviour, move on and try again to be better the next time. You will make mistakes; you will fail, but you can choose to forgive, to learn and stand up again. Nobody is perfect, but as long as we are learning we are growing. Learn from the past, look to the future, and live in the now.

I have given the past too much significance, and because I am a dreamer and a planner, I tend to get lost in the future and completely forget about the here and now.

I mean, don't get me wrong – I think your dreams and visions for the future are so important. They will help you move forward, but don't forget that your actions now define your future and that you need to be confident and happy in the now. When I heard the quote by John C Maxwell (online conference, 2nd May 2020, Rise x Live), "We overestimate the future and we exaggerate the past, but underestimate the now," I realised what truth lay within his words. I want you to really think about this statement, let go of the past and live more in the now.

CREATING MEMORIES

I strongly believe in creating positive memories. Memories that will outshine the things that haven't gone right or may not go right in the future. Memories of love and laughter, memories of togetherness. I remember very clearly how my mum, my sister and I used to dance together in the living room. Looking back now, I don't actually think we did it that often, but it has left such a positive memory and impact on me. Now I often do the same with my kids.

Obviously, our love of travelling or taking short trips helps create great memories for us as a family. I love to create a photo book for every trip we take, and the kids love looking at them and talk about that particular holiday.

The other day Maximilian said to me that he was thinking of our trip to Ethiopia. It was a holiday that was totally back to the basics; we hiked and had no running water or electricity half the time. Together we saw a different way of life and we spent time as a family without the daily distractions of phones or tablets; we did not even have toys with us. The kids may not remember everything later in life, but we will all remember some things. He talked about events I don't even remember, but that somehow had left an impression on him. What they will remember is how they spent time with us; they will remember the exciting experiences, the scary ones and the ones that made them truly happy.

I also believe we create memories through seemingly less important everyday things, like our family rituals and traditions. Things like having dinner together or our family's way of celebrating a birthday in the house. Every night we remember the positive, fun and memorable events that happened during the day. Gordon and I try to spend a lot of one-on-one time with the kids, and we do small things, such as going for a bike ride or having an ice cream together. Creating memories does not have to be something you do all the time; it does not need to cost any money or take up a lot of time. It's the ordinary, small things that become important and create those feel-good memories – like dancing in the living room.

Every summer, we fly to Germany, to the same place, to spend time with the grandparents and the rest of the family. This is one of the main reasons I have never really considered working for a company again. It is the reason why I stay self-employed. It gives me the freedom to spend the summers in my home country with my children. It also gives me the opportunity to create wonderful memories there. We have created a home, a base and stability, which is something I feel is missing in our expat life. Creating these memories are not just for myself: I know how important they will be for the kids, in so many ways, when they are older.

I HAVE LEARNED THAT LETTING GO OF THE PAST IS MY CHOICE:

1. Accepting a label or a definition created for me by someone else is something I can choose not to do or be.

2. Forgiveness is my choice.

3. Remembering the positives is my choice.

4. Not allowing myself to repeat the same mistakes is my choice.

5. Living in the now, looking into the future and creating memories in the now is my choice.

CHAPTER FOUR

OTHER PEOPLE'S OPINIONS ARE NOT YOURS

When I was younger, I wanted to be a fashion designer. There was just one problem: I thought I couldn't draw. One day I saw an ad on the train about a university in my hometown that was teaching fashion management. It was a private university. I was on the underground with one of my best friends who, in my mind, knew a lot. She always seemed to be right. So, when she saw me gazing at this ad, she said, "A university that has to pay for ads on the underground and a university you have to pay to attend is not good." My very short-lived dream of going to that university was shattered with that one sentence. I never even told my parents or anybody else about it. That is how much I allowed myself to be influenced by others.

A few years later, a good friend of mine went to that university and I met someone else who had been there years before. It was not new, and it is still around now. I went to my friend's final fashion show and absolutely loved what I saw, the atmosphere and the show. It would have been the perfect university for me.

I don't think that my friend even remembers this moment. Nor does she know how much she influenced me. Needless to say, I didn't study fashion design. I did business studies instead. Something that was definitely not right for me. But something that seemed right in everyone else's opinion. You can't go wrong with business studies, right?

I buried my dreams because of other people's opinions. And I don't want you to make the same mistake. If you have already done it, I want you to know that it is not too late. You can still change your decisions.

I look back now and wonder how other people could have influenced me so much. Nobody can influence me now, at least not to such an extent that I would allow myself to change my life plans. I used to listen to other people all the time. I thought they knew better; I thought I didn't know anything or that my opinion wasn't as good as theirs. I was afraid to share my own opinion, which definitely made me a people-pleaser.

I do it differently now. Gordon often says to me, "Why do you ask? You won't listen anyway." No, I may not. I don't ask because I don't have my own opinion or won't listen to my own heart. I ask because I want a different perspective. I want to learn or understand everything about the situation. Maybe there are things I haven't thought about or haven't seen myself. Once I have heard opinions, I evaluate them and then make my own decision.

There is a huge difference.

Whether you ask other people for opinions or whether you get their opinions without asking – that happens a lot too, as we all know. My advice is take what is important for you or what makes sense to you and your life and forget about the rest. Listen to their opinions but do not let their opinions second-guess your own if you believe differently. Remember, it is your life, not theirs.

The thing with other people's opinions is that they are THEIR opinions, not yours. Their opinions may work for their lives, but not for yours. They don't have to live with that decision; they will not be the ones who fail or succeed. They may even forget about their advice and opinion the minute they leave the room.

When I decided to start my website design business, a friend told me that it was the wrong decision. She gave me many reasons why it would not work – in her opinion. There are so many graphic designers out there who are a lot cheaper. The competition is huge and cheap. Everyone is online these days and many offer affordable services on online platforms. And yes, she was right. If it had been my younger self, the one who believed that everyone else's opinion was more important than my own, I would have stopped right there. I would have thought, "She knows more about that industry." She had her own ideas of what I could achieve or what I was capable of. These ideas were based on her own experiences, something she would like for her industry.

I won't go into detail, but what is important, first, is that she didn't mean it negatively. She meant well. Second, yes, her idea for me may have been a good one in general at that moment, and she may have thought that I would be good at it. Her opinions had nothing to do with my reality, and I believed in my idea.

Why do so many of us need other people's approval to do the things we want to do? Why do we so often want to please our parents, even when we are parents ourselves? I mean, I am so guilty of this. I still catch myself wanting approval from other people, especially my family, for my actions, behaviour or decisions. I feel hurt when they disapprove. Have you ever caught yourself calling your parents, your partner or a friend, asking for advice when in fact you just wanted their approval? Well, I have. Even though I know I don't need it. Even though I am confident. Even though I am proud of myself when I know I have done something well.

My dad raised me to believe that praise was the most important reward, so I tried to receive praise to feel worthy and loved by him. However, I received it only when I achieved the things that he thought were right. We received money when we got an A for certain subjects that he believed were important – not PE, art or religion; no money for those subjects. I don't know what it is like when you are an only child, but when there is more than one child it is so obvious. Everyone is fighting for the attention and praise from their parents. We did it as kids, and now I see it in my kids as well. Every child is different of course, but I tried to do what was expected of me and even better to get the praise and the love I wanted from my parents.

I now know that my praise for myself, my own approval of myself, is most important.

WHAT YOU THINK OF ME IS NONE OF MY BUSINESS

There are many books about this topic and one of them even has this exact title, because it is so true. Other people's opinions are their opinions and have nothing to do with you. Everyone is a free person and can think what they want to think. It is up to you whether you let it affect you. I found this concept such a revelation. It is all up to me. Whether I listen to other people's opinions about my actions, achievements, dreams, desires and choices, whether I let them affect me or not, it is up to me. It is my choice.

People in general think about themselves first and what is in it for them. So, people's opinions about you are not actually about you: it is about themselves. They are thinking these thoughts; they have these opinions because they will benefit from it. It may make them feel better. Just as I tried to make myself feel better when I judged other people. It may make them appear better to other people. Or it may just be a distraction from their own unhappiness or inability. Whatever the reason for their opinion or judgment, it has nothing to do with you. Nobody else is responsible for your life. Nobody else will live your life. The other people will not be there when you fail, and they will not be there when you succeed. You are responsible for your life. And you are not responsible for their life.

As I said before, this thought has helped me a lot, ever since I heard it; many times it has helped me ground myself and focus back on myself.

CHANGING PERSPECTIVE

Sometimes, however, this knowledge is not enough, and I have learned other ways of dealing with people's opinions. I change perspective.

Perspective is the way you see things, events and people. How you perceive and feel about them. And that is determined by your own experiences and learnings. We can look at the same thing, situation or person, and feel totally different about it from the way others do. We all look at it from a different perspective, with ourselves in mind. When my daughter Felicia sees a cat, she runs away, because she is so scared of cats. She had a bad experience with a cat when she was very little, and since then her perception of cats is that they are something dangerous. Gordon looks at cats and gets out the watering hose, wanting them to go away. He sees only that the cats are lying on his garden furniture and their hair is everywhere; he sees cats as a nuisance. When my friend, who grew up with many cats, looks at them, she sees the cutest animals and wants to hug them.

Here's another example of perspective: when I look at an aeroplane, I think that I am glad I am not sitting in it. I see it as something uncomfortable, but when our friend looks at aeroplanes, he finds it exciting. He wants to find out what model it is and where it will be flying to. Gordon looks at an aeroplane and thinks of travelling, which is exciting, but sitting on the aeroplane is boring, because it usually takes up a lot of his time. When my kids think of an aeroplane, all they see is unlimited film time and feel excited. As you can see, everyone has a different view of things, because of how they have experienced that situation, thing, animal or person. It's their perspective.

The great thing about perspective is that because it is determined by our own experiences, and nobody else's, we can change it. We can change how we view a situation or a person.

When I feel judged by someone or feel that someone else's opinion is weighing me down and it is not enough to tell myself that their opinion is not my business, I change my perspective. I put myself in their shoes and think, "Why they would say something like that. What was their intention? Where do they stand in life? Are they making a valid point? Or are they saying these things because of their own experiences in the past, which have nothing to do with me? Are they actually thinking about themselves? Is there anything they could gain by telling me that opinion?"

I could easily have been influenced by my friend who told me that I would never succeed in becoming a website designer. She had been working in Dubai for a long time, she knew the market and it seemed as though she was right. You know the way people talk, and they just make everyone feel they are absolutely right. However, I changed my perspective and put myself in her shoes and realised her opinion had nothing to do with me. She did not know me or my dreams. She didn't really know why I wanted to be a website designer and what differentiated me from my competitors. She was sharing her opinion, formed by looking at her own life. Her competition in her industry. How she could have needed me. She was not considering my life.

BEING FREE

I want to be free rather than worry about what others think.

My mum was one of the most confident people I knew, growing up. To this day, I don't think I have met anybody else who was that confident in a positive way and cared so little about other people's opinions. She truly did not care. And she lived a totally free life because of it. She was truly herself and truly happy.

This confidence made her hugely attractive and successful. I think that she also intimidated some people who did not know her well – maybe even scared them a bit.

She did whatever she wanted. She would cycle to school barefoot to drop us off and did not think anything of it. It was only until one mum pointed out that she admired her so much for her confidence that she herself realised that this was something others couldn't do, just because of people's opinions. She would say what she wanted to say and stand up for herself in any situation. It was certainly not the easiest way, but she was true to herself.

Needless to say, I admired her hugely and often wondered why I turned out so differently.

For her it was not a choice; she was somehow just born that way. Or was she raised that way? I don't know. It took me a long time to achieve the level of confidence that she had. I am not even sure I am there yet. I am working on it. However, for me it was a choice I had to make. I worked on not caring about other people's opinions. I challenged myself again and again, and I still do.

By the way, there is always someone who does things better than you, someone who is more helpful, someone who works harder, someone who is more dedicated. And there will always be a more confident person than you. That is good! It means there is always something to learn and something to strive for.

Even in my mum's case, there was a woman at our sports club that she admired. This woman was an actress and really did not care about other people's opinions. And people had a lot of opinions about her. She was pretty, she was confident and she had a great body, which she wasn't afraid of showing off. I still remember: she would wear very short skirts, sometimes white and almost see-through, and that's how she would cycle around our neighbourhood and the conservative sports club. I guess you can imagine what people said – let's put it this way, it was not always positive. But my mum admired her for being herself and not caring about other people's opinions. And looking back now, I do too.

Making the choice to not care about other people's opinions and not being influenced by them makes you free. Free to do what you like. Free to say what you want to say. Free to wear what you love to wear and, most importantly, free to live your life and nobody else's.

EVERYBODY HAS AN OPINION

But that doesn't mean they are right.

When you Google the word 'opinion', the first thing that comes up is 'a view or judgment formed about something, not necessarily based on facts or knowledge'.

Everybody has opinions and so many people feel the urge to share theirs. What you need to remember is that, just because someone shares an opinion, it doesn't mean they are right: it is just their view. Who determines who is right or wrong? Often there is no right or wrong answer. There is just an opinion based on certain experiences.

I had my first two kids in America. I knew nothing about kids and babies, and I learned everything there. I mean everything about pregnancy, about birth, about breastfeeding, postnatal depression, how to bathe a baby (when and how often), how to get them to sleep, when to start solids, what to start them on – and the list is endless. If you are a mum, you know what I mean. It is like going to university again; there is so much to learn.

The thing is I learned it all the American way and it made sense to me. I followed the guidelines and my son was surviving. I mean he was not just surviving: he was thriving. He was growing and he was a happy baby. He got his first teeth and he started to eat solids – very messy, but he did – and I learned how to get him to sleep.

He was seven months old when I took him home to Germany for his first summer holiday. AND all the opinions started! I'm sure you can picture the situation. "Why is he sitting in a chair when he can't sit up by himself?" "What are you feeding him?" "Why is he eating carrots, not porridge, for dinner?"

When I had two kids and went to Germany for the summer, it was the same. I heard about so many things that I was doing wrong. "How can you cook a hot meal for dinner?" "Two hot meals a day? No bread? No wonder the Americans are so fat." The list went on and on. I don't remember everything, but I can tell you, there was an overflow of opinions.

I guess you don't even have to go to another country to feel overwhelmed by all the information and well-meant advice. It comes from all sides – friends, other mums you meet randomly, grandparents (often specifically the grandmothers), nurses, shop assistants, books, magazines, blogs, YouTube, I mean literally everywhere. And people just don't stop. Yes, I asked for opinions and got some great tips, but there were times that I didn't ask and received many unwanted opinions.

That is why I have stopped listening to other people's opinions about how I raise my kids. I listen to myself. Nobody else defines me as a mum, apart from myself and the love for my kids.

And nobody else defines you. Only YOU define yourself.

LISTEN TO YOUR GUT

The best advice I got when I had kids was from my mum. "Listen to your gut. You will know. You will feel when something is right and when something is wrong." My mum said when we were babies the 'rules' were different and we all grew up just fine and are all healthy. So, I started doing that. I used the things I had learned in America that I liked and that worked for us and I used the things I liked from Germany. However, the voices of these opinionated people didn't stop until I had outnumbered them by having more children. I seemed to be doing something right. My kids seem to be fine so far.

I use this advice not only for raising my kids, but all the time, and in many different aspects of my life. And this practice has not disappointed me. The feeling in my stomach, my intuition, is usually right. It is like the Indian saying, "We listen with our brain; we feel with our heart and we decide with our gut."

THINGS THAT HAVE HELPED ME

These are my six lessons that have helped me to not listen to other people, to become more confident and just do my own thing:

1. Realise that other people don't really think or care about you. People are concerned with their own lives. They think about themselves. Especially the ones you don't know. This may sound super hard, but it is what I have come to realise. I would say 90 per cent of the people in your circle don't really care. They are quick to share an opinion without even thinking about it. Remember, if that person had to make the decision for their own life, they would probably do it differently anyway.

2. The 10 per cent that do care, are still not you. They don't really know what you want or like. They have their own agenda. Let's say your parents, of course they care and have your best interest at heart, but they also have their own ideas for you. They have their opinion about what is good for you. They want you to be safe, happy and healthy. Probably have a lot of money (as that brings a form of safety – and is supposed to make everyone feel happy). BUT they don't have your dreams. Remember you are unique, with your own experiences, goals and dreams.

3. Make gut decisions and see. I'm a super strong believer in the gut. If you think you don't have a gut feeling, go and dig deeper. There is always a gut feeling. Maybe you will find it through meditation. Sitting in silence and really listening to my inner self, digging deeper into my subconscious, often helps me see more clearly. Another tool I use is to talk to someone about my issue and hear them out. By listening, I notice subconsciously how my body is feeling when different opinions are raised. My gut feeling is telling me something.

Learn to listen to your gut, follow your instincts, realise the outcome and how it is right. Practise it, use a small issue and follow your gut. See what happens and whether your gut feeling was right.

4. Ask yourself: Why should someone else know better than I? We all have ideas about everything. We have so much information coming at us from social media, news, people, everywhere. Our opinions and ideas are formed by our own experiences – what does this mean? It means that your opinion is different from mine because we live different lives. Form your own opinion before you listen to someone else: do your own research. Experience everything yourself; try things yourself. Then you can really know!

5. Put yourself in their shoes. If you are finding it hard to block out other people's voices, change your perspective and think, "Why did they say that? Are they making a valid point? Or are they seeing it with blurred vision because of their own negative or positive experiences? Are they thinking about themselves? Why are they saying what they are saying?" Understand them better to understand whether or not they have a point.

6. And remember Chapter 2 – Judging. Judging happens all the time. It can be upsetting, but remember that people who judge are often insecure, jealous, angry or have some issue within themselves. It is usually about them, not about you. At the end of the day, you can make the choice and not listen. The choice not to let them influence you. The choice to live your life instead of allowing other people to limit you. The choice to believe in yourself. The choice to walk away. The choice to look for other friends. You have a choice.

I HAVE LEARNED THAT NOT LISTENING TO OTHER PEOPLE'S OPINIONS IS A CHOICE:

1. I have the choice to believe in myself and in my own abilities. Nobody can tell me how to live MY life.

2. I listen, I evaluate, I take what is right for me and my life and I forget about the rest.

3. Other people are not responsible for my life. They may have their opinion, but they don't have to live my life. They are not there when I fail, and they are not there when I succeed.

4. Other people's opinions are theirs and none of my business.

5. My beliefs are not true for everyone and vice versa. They are just opinions.

CHAPTER FIVE

OTHER PEOPLE
ARE NOT BETTER THAN YOU

Other people are not prettier, more intelligent, faster, better mums or better people than you are. And you are not better than anybody else. When you think about it, really take time to think about this: we are all the same. We may differ in appearance and have different strengths, behaviours, perceptions, fears and judgments. We most certainly will have different interests and ways of living, but one is not better than the other. Essentially, we are all humans with a desire for love, safety and shelter. We are all similar. As mentioned before, the one thing I have definitely learned from living in Dubai, with people of so many different nationalities, religions, beliefs, values and backgrounds, is that we are actually all similar. We have problems, fears and sorrows, and we have joys and happiness.

Everyone is born and everyone dies. Everything else you choose to do in between is your choice, but it is not better or worse than anybody else's choice: it is your choice. Everyone is trying to figure out this thing called life.

In my 'mum' life, I often have destructive thoughts, such as, "I am a horrible mum." I make mistakes, I don't stay calm and end up screaming at the kids. We have all been there. Wishing we had paid more attention when they wanted to tell you something important and we were busy doing something else. I wish I had reacted in a different way, when instead I was triggered by my kids' behaviour. To tell you the truth, I am very good at beating myself up afterwards. I make it up to my kids. I am better the next time or the next day, but most of the time that horrible voice in my head telling me I am a bad mum won't let go. I am learning to forgive myself, let it go and move on. I am learning to acknowledge what happened and make better choices the next time. Every single day.

I remember my son Maximilian, then one and a half years old, falling head first down the stairs. I had let him crawl away while changing my second son, thinking he would not be so fast. When I looked up, he was by the stairs; I ran over, but I was too late. He lost his balance and fell. I saw it all, in slow motion time lapse. If I close my eyes now, I can still see it happening. He fell head first, halfway down, landed on his head on one step and continued to fall all the way down. I screamed the most horrific scream I had ever screamed in my life. At that moment, I honestly didn't believe he could survive that fall. But by some miracle, he had only a tiny scratch on his forehead. He must have had all his angels watching over him.

My whole family learned a lesson that day: nobody ever had stairs without protection again.

A few months later, when I was alone with the kids in Germany, my second son put a piece of plastic into his mouth and started choking on it. I had let him bite on a packet of tissue papers because he was teething, and he loved it so much. What I hadn't thought about was the little flap that covered the opening. When I looked at the packet again, I realised the plastic bit was missing. I searched everywhere, in his mouth, where he had been playing and I could not find it. As he seemed totally happy, I convinced myself that the little plastic flap had not been on the package in the first place. Shortly afterwards, he started choking and I became really frightened. I started hitting him on the back, as we we had learned in baby CPR (cardiopulmonary resuscitation) training, realising at the same time that this was a flat piece of plastic and not a proper piece of something like a carrot, and that it was pointless. My son started turning blue. I totally panicked and frantically searched for the emergency number in Germany. By the time I found it, my son had stopped choking and had started breathing normally again. He was a happy camper. I called our paediatrician and told her what had happened. She explained to me that there were two possible scenarios: he could have swallowed it and it would come out the normal way in a few days; I just needed to keep checking his dirty nappies. Or it could have gone down the airway into his lungs. I went and had him checked out, and his lungs sounded normal. By the time the piece of plastic reappeared a whole week later in his dirty nappy, I had already convinced myself that he had not swallowed anything. But I can't tell you what a relief it was to see this tiny piece reappear.

The paediatrician told me that this was one of the top choking hazards for babies. It didn't make me feel any better, to be honest.

What I want to say with these stories is that crazy, scary situations happen and luckily in 99 per cent of cases they turn out positive. They do not make you a better or worse mum. We are all trying to do our best in raising these little humans. Sometimes we fail; sometimes we succeed. Most importantly, we are learning and getting better.

And again, it depends on our perspective. Our babies grow up in different parts of the world and we raise them in different ways, but they grow up. It does not make us better or worse than other mums from different countries.

A totally different story but the same lesson learned was that for a long time I thought that other people could just do things better than I could and that I would never be able to learn them. I often found myself feeling jealous when looking at other runners. They seem to run faster and longer, with less training. I believed that I was not built for running. I thought they were better than me because of it. However, other people just have different talents. Some have the physique to be fast runners, some have an aptitude for cooking, some are natural musicians, while other people are great with animals.

We are all born with some natural talents. Everyone's talent is different. And when someone is better at something, it doesn't mean they are better in general; it doesn't make them a better person. They just find it easier to learn, but if you want, you can learn it as well. You may just need a little longer and you may not be as good, but you can learn anything. And by the way, someone else can have all the talent in the world, but if they don't train and you train every day and have the willpower, you will most likely be better than them at that particular thing.

FITTING IN

Why do people follow trends and groups and other people? Are they afraid of missing out? Do they think fitting in will make them happier? I think there is a big difference between like-minded people and being part of a trend or joining a group of people in order to be happier or more confident.

I've been there. I tried to fit in because I thought it would make me happy. And I have seen it in so many other people and friends. For myself, I am so happy that this never lasted long. And I think this is mostly due to my mum, who kept on instilling in us that we were enough, that we didn't need status or certain brands or a certain behaviour or to be part of certain groups in order to be happy or to be accepted.

This is particularly true when you are a teenager, but I also hear those stories from adults. Grown women who want to fit in. And they want their kids to fit in. Some wear certain types of clothes, own a house in a certain area and furnish it a certain way; some want to be part of a certain group of friends, and some need to travel to specific holiday destinations. And don't get me wrong – there is nothing wrong with this as long as you do it for the right reasons and not in the hope of feeling better or to be something or someone that you actually don't feel like being. If you can relate to any of the above, promise me that you will ask yourself, "Is this really me? What do I really want?"

I once heard a mum make the comment, "He's so cool, of course the other kids want to play with him," during a playdate at our local park. What she didn't say, but what was obvious, was that the third kid playing with them was not as cool in appearance or the way he acted, so it was no wonder he was a bit of an outsider. It took a while for this to sink in. I was a little speechless. This mum was already training her son to choose which kids were cool, and somehow better, and which ones were not. Aside from labelling others, she was telling her son subconsciously that he needed to be cool to fit in.

This incident made me even more conscious of the kind of words I use in front of my kids. I do not want to label my children and I definitely do not want to label other people. The interesting part of this particular story is that the boy who was referred to as cool was actually not as self-confident as the child who was not as cool but who was at ease with himself. And I can only hope for him, that he stays this way.

THE LIES WE TELL OURSELVES ABOUT OUR BODIES

Entwined with confidence, especially for women, is our body or body perception. Women have so many insecurities about their own bodies, not only as teenagers, but well into adult life. When it comes to their own bodies, women find it very easy to criticise, to find things that are wrong. Women keep comparing themselves to others and the bodies of other women are always better.

I read an article in a magazine that really struck me. It was about body image and how so many young girls are not happy about their body. The question was, "What would you change about your body if you could change anything?" The girls talked about their freckles, their thighs, their hair, their arms and being too big in general. Every girl in the article had something they were not happy about.

And what affected me even more were the statistics presented alongside the article: almost half of all 15-year-old girls think they are too fat. Anorexia is still the highest cause of mortality in girls (facts from *Emotion magazine 11-2019*). And on the ANAD (National Association of Anorexia Nervosa and Associated Disorders) website it says, "Eating disorders have the highest mortality rate of any mental illness."

I haven't even started digging into this, but these numbers are already shocking to me.

So many young girls are concerned about their bodies and aspects they consider not right or not pretty. And as I said, it doesn't stop in young girls. I thought of the RISE women's conference, which I went to in the summer of 2019. We were asked to stand up if we were or ever had been unhappy about our bodies. And probably every woman, 3,000 women, in that room stood up.

Why are we so concerned about our bodies? Why do we spend so much time thinking about our bodies? We could use this time in a much better way if we just forgot about our bodies and focused on something else instead. How much could we achieve if we just thought about other things, positive things about ourselves, our dreams, plans, ideas and goals?

We think to ourselves things about our bodies (and anything else for that matter) that we would never say to anybody. And nobody would dare say that to our face either. I am saying 'we' because even though I feel very confident about my body now, I do admit I still think about it, just as you probably do. Not as much anymore, but I do from time to time.

Naively, I somehow assumed that young girls these days are not as concerned about their bodies and how they look as my generation was when we were young. I assumed there had been so much in the media about how wrong the size 0 for models is that all these body issues were not so relevant anymore. I assumed there was so much more accessible help and motivation out there, and that young girls were a lot more confident these days. Confident with themselves and their bodies. I thought that the focus was on inner strength and beauty and not so much on the looks anymore.

I kind of forgot to think about Instagram and social media and all the filters that are out there and the effect this has on young girls. The lies that it tells all women out there. I may have forgotten that being a teenager is a difficult time, overall, and that other women may find it as difficult as I did to accept themselves. Regardless of the age or the century. Regardless of the country they live in or the religion they believe in.

MY OWN STORY ABOUT MY BODY

When I read the article, it triggered something in me. I was so shocked, because I was like that for so many years. When I was a teenager, I was so unhappy about my body. I was tall and skinny, and looking back now, I guess there were other people who envied me and my body. I could eat all I wanted and did not put on weight. All I could think about were my flaws, especially my small boobs. I hated to get changed for PE, I did not like wearing bathing suits and I started walking hunched forward. My dad kept pulling my shoulders back and kept telling me I would never be able to walk straight again. I did not care, all I wanted was to hide my body.

When I was about 14, I started to take the pill in the hope that the extra hormones would make my body curvier and I would look more like other girls. It did not help. And, of course, I thought I would never have a boyfriend looking the way I did. For me everything started to be about my body. I was very critical. I was concerned about the freckles on my face, my small eyes, my short eyelashes, my big fingers and my short legs. However, most of my attention went to my cup size and how unfair it was and how much I could not have, do and wear because of that.

I began to obsess about what other people might think or say. Of how I looked in certain clothes, what I could wear or not. I hated looking at myself in the mirror. The problem was not other people making fun of me, although that has happened: the problem was me and what that voice in my head was saying.

I thought about plastic surgery and about having breast implants, but I was too scared to follow through. Too scared of surgery, but the irony was that I was also too scared of the outcome and what other people might say. What other people might think. Again, it was about the other people and their opinions about me. I was worried what people thought about my small boobs and I was worried what they would say of the sudden change because of surgery. Totally crazy in retrospect. But it is the truth.

Looking back, I wonder how much time I wasted worrying about my body and about other people's thoughts. How much this issue held me back.

I guess somewhere deep down I knew that confidence came from the inside and not because of the way I looked or how I was like other people. I guess I knew that once I learned to love myself the way I was, my insecurities would go away.

It took me many years to fully realise how little people actually notice other people. Looking back, almost nobody talked about me and my body. I really noticed it when I was pregnant with my last baby. I walked around my kids' school with a huge belly, I saw other parents every day and some only noticed the pregnancy when I was about nine months pregnant. I even had one mum congratulate me, totally surprised by the birth of my daughter, saying that she never noticed anything. What that shows me is that people don't actually look at other people as much as we think – they are too engaged in their own lives and problems, too engaged in worrying about their own flaws and judging themselves. Don't be that hard on yourself!

WHAT I WANT TO SAY TO MY YOUNGER SELF – AND OTHERS

Now that I am older and very confident about myself and my body, I just want to hug the little girl I was and all the other girls who are ashamed of aspects of their bodies and want to look like someone else. I want to tell myself that it is going to be OK; you will grow up to be a confident woman. You will have boyfriends who love you regardless, you will have a loving husband who loves your body the way it is and the way it develops. I want to tell myself that you are going to grow up and become a strong and confident woman who is going to run half-marathons and even do Half Ironman races with that body. You will be a woman who will be pregnant four times, deliver four babies and breastfeed them all. In fact, you will breastfeed for a total of almost eight years and give your kids a great start to their lives. This body will do so many amazing things.

I learned only much later that there are so many women out there with larger breasts who cannot breastfeed. I took it for granted and was very fortunate that I never had major breastfeeding problems.

In my thoughts, I am hugging my younger self and all you girls and women. Let me tell those of you who are so worried about your bodies – your body is amazing. Your body can do amazing things. It does not matter what you look like, it does not matter if you are a size 4 or 12 or 20. It does not matter if you have curly hair or straight hair, or if you are short or tall. It does not matter if your bum or your boobs are big or small. It does not matter whether you can breastfeed or not, whether you deliver a baby via C-section or naturally, or if you can't have a baby at all. Nobody else is better than you. You are the way you are, and you are beautiful and strong.

It is good that we are all different; the world would be so boring if we were all the same.

Ask yourself, if you were to make a list of all the people you love, where would you be on that list?

Your worth does not depend on other people, a boyfriend or a husband. You need to love yourself first. It does not matter what other people think. They most probably don't even think about you. And even if they do, remember their opinion of you is none of your business.

And when someone else does comment on your body, remind yourself it probably comes from their own insecurities about themselves; so, ignore, forgive and move on. Feel compassion for the other person for their insecurities and for needing to comment on other people. I know it is hard in the beginning, but with a little practice it will become easier.

Look into the mirror every day and tell yourself how beautiful and strong you are. Tell yourself how many amazing things your body has done and can still do. Don't ever allow anyone else to tell you how your body should look. And don't ever say things to yourself that you would never say to anyone else.

A friend of mine asked when my own body insecurities stopped. How long they lasted into adulthood. I can't really pinpoint a time when I became confident in my own body or how I did it. It took time and I did so many different things. My family helped, therapy helped, my friends helped, my boyfriends helped (yes, a little validation from the outside helps of course), having children helped, becoming confident through other things – like sport, for me – helped, moving countries helped, getting different perspectives helped and just growing up and growing out of the teenage years helped. It took time to become confident in my own body. However, I did. And so will you.

There is always a way; you just have to go and look for it.

Once you realise that nobody else is better than you and that you are not better than anybody else, you will feel less judged and you will judge less too.

I HAVE LEARNED THAT THAT OTHERS ARE NOT BETTER THAN ME AND I AM NOT BETTER THAN OTHERS:

1. I know that I am already perfect within myself; everybody is perfect just the way they are.

2. My body confidence comes from the inside, not through the validation of others.

3. I choose to do things my way. My way may be different, but not better or worse than other people's ways.

4. Staying firm in my own beliefs and dreams brings me confidence.

5. Other people don't think of me, they think of themselves.

CHAPTER SIX

THE TRUTH IS NOT ALL FRIENDS ARE GOOD FOR YOUR LIFE

We become who we surround ourselves with.

Has anyone ever told you that you look like your husband? Or maybe you have seen couples who look like each other. Have you ever caught yourself thinking that two friends look more like sisters than friends?

It has happened a few times here in Dubai to me and my best friend – people assumed we were sisters. Thinking back, it happened to me at school as well.

Friends tend to wear similar clothes or styles of clothes. They decorate their homes in a similar fashion, listen to similar music and even have similar tastes in food.

Certainly, with teenagers and in general within groups of friends, there are always fashion rules or codes. I often see a group of friends who wear similar things, and all look the same. Not too long ago I got a picture from my brother's holiday and I could hardly recognise him. All the young men looked the same to me. They had on similar T-shirts, sunglasses, hairstyles, beards and shoes.

You don't adapt only your looks consciously or subconsciously when you spend a lot of time with someone. It is also true for behaviour, interests, likes and dislikes. And now that I am sitting here, thinking about it and writing about it, I can see so many instances of my friends and I being similar, and the same is true for other groups of friends.

Of course, that is also why friendships and partnerships work; we have similar tastes. That's why we have something to talk about and something to do together.

I have always been active. However, because I married a man who is fanatical (almost) and very competitive about sports, I have become more active. We push each other, we hold each other to account and we motivate each other. If Gordon were the opposite, or not as interested in sport, would it be as easy for me to train every day? I don't think so.

The same is true for food (and alcohol for that matter). My friend Ilse is a nutritionist, and because we spend a lot of time together and talk about her passion, I am influenced by her. I already had a general interest in healthy eating, but because I can, I ask her a lot of questions and I learn more. The more I become interested, the more I subconsciously surround myself with others who are interested in healthy nutrition, online on social media and offline.

And the cycle goes on. I am conscious of what I am eating. Gordon and everyone around me sees it and is subsequently influenced. Although he may not adapt to everything, my behaviour has an impact on him. Gordon and I hardly drink any alcohol anymore; in all seriousness, we drink alcohol only when we go out. And that is partly because of our exercise routine, but partly also because we influence each other. If I want to have a drink and Gordon says no, because he wants to get up early the next day to train, I would probably also not pour myself a drink – after all, it is not much fun to drink alone.

At the beginning of the year, I decided that I wanted to try out the vegan lifestyle, and Gordon went along. If you knew him and his meat addiction, you would never believe he agreed to this. And I doubt he would have done that without me. But it happened gradually. I have always eaten very little meat; my son and I are lactose intolerant and I have not bought real milk or much cheese in years. The step for me to become a vegan was a tiny one. For Gordon it was bigger, but he had been watching me for a long time and was obviously influenced.

The same is true for behaviour. Adapting a behaviour doesn't happen overnight: it happens gradually. And often without you really noticing.

When my university friend Anna was in hospital and I spent so much time with her other friend, Julia, I was clearly influenced by her and I'm not proud of it to say the least. However, we spent so much time together that I adapted. It was not good for me, which I did not see at the time, but I saw it very clearly later on. You adapt to the people you spend time with.

LOOK AT YOUR FRIENDSHIPS

Not all friends are good for you. I hate to say this, but it's the truth: stay away from toxic friendships and relationships. If a friendship does not feel right anymore for you, if it is dragging you down rather than uplifting you, you can choose to walk away. And by the way, this is not only true for friends but people in general, maybe even family, even your husband or wife.

I had to cut some people out of my life completely. And yes, it was very hard. One was an ex-boyfriend who broke my heart and then tried to stay in touch. I protected myself, my broken heart and my sanity by cutting him out and concentrating on the future and my life without him, rather than constantly being thrown backwards and spiralling down into sad feelings. To this day, I don't really understand why he kept calling me and why he tried to stay in contact, even when he had a new girlfriend. I know it happens all the time, both ways.

There are multiple reasons why people act this way: they may still have feelings for the other person, or they want to keep the possibility of hooking up again if something goes wrong with their new relationship. They may just be worried and feel responsible for the other person, or even just want to feel needed. Whatever the reason, I would say if you have been hurt or treated badly by someone in the past, stay away from that person. Stay away to protect yourself. It may be hard; it was very hard for me. And it did take me some time, but once I cut him out of my life, it was much easier to move on.

Another person I had to cut the cord with was a friend. She wanted a version of friendship that I could not return. She wanted me to be her friend, and her friend only. I have many friends and am happy about it. None of my other friends understood why we were even close. She seemed very negative towards others and although I could see where my friends were coming from, I still tried and stayed loyal to her for a long time. One day, the accusations got too much, and I realised that being around her only dragged me down and put unnecessary pressure on me. I decided not to react to her complaining messages anymore. Out of loyalty, and maybe also pity, I tried a few times to keep the friendship alive, until I realised it was just not good for me. In her opinion, I did not behave as a good friend should behave. In my opinion, we did not have the same understanding of a friendship and, to be honest, I have so many better friends that I did not need to hold on to something that was just negative for me. To me this friendship did not feel right anymore, so I decided to let go.

Last, I walked away from an unhealthy business partner. It was a very hard time, because I felt I had been treated unfairly and in a way that I would never treat other people myself. The decision to leave also meant I lost a lot of money. But losing that money was worth it for my own sanity. In retrospect, I would say it came down to having a different understanding of what we wanted out of that business and why we started. We also had a different understanding of how to treat people and how to do business. Once I had left, I felt so relieved, although there were all these unclear issues about money between us. In order to protect myself, I cut her out of my life. Looking back now, I can see the positives, as I have learned many lessons out of that relationship. One was to never have a business partner without a contract. The other was that I have to set my boundaries more clearly; I have to speak up right from the beginning; and I have to stay true to my life and my dreams. I realised that people can treat me badly only if I allow them to.

Being in my early 40s, I am now at an age where divorces are happening in my circle of friends. It can be horrible, especially when kids are involved. I am the last person who says "Go, leave your partner." I am always for the trying. However, I also hear so many stories where it is obviously not working. They have tried many things, but one person in the relationship stays unhappy or unsatisfied. I have heard stories of one partner being ignored by the other, screamed at continually or, even worse, beaten. And all I can think is, "Why are you not leaving? Why do you stay in that relationship? It does not make you happy."

I know that not every woman thinks she is financially able to leave her husband. This is such a huge topic that it could fill another book on its own. I included this part here because I want to make everyone think. Regardless of your situation, you still always have a choice. If a relationship is so toxic, you can choose to leave and start again financially. It may not be easy; it may be less 'secure', but you can leave. To every action there is a consequence. Sometimes we know the consequences of our action in advance and sometimes not. However, every action we take is our choice. Not taking any action is also a choice. You can choose to act and deal with the consequences.

The second thought I have is that I do not want this to happen to my kids. I want to teach my kids to be strong and independent. I may have been shy and lacked confidence, but I was raised in a way that I would never ever allow anyone to treat me badly over a long period of time without leaving. And that's something I want to pass on to my kids. I do not want to see my kids grow up and stay in a relationship where they are unhappy. And this is true for any kind of relationship. And if money is the reason for staying, it is by far not as important as happiness. And while many parents say that, not everybody acts that way. Too often I have heard parents say things like, "Oh, just try a little harder," or "You have to be nicer to your partner." NO, you don't have to try harder, you have to be confident, you have to speak up and stand up for yourself. People treat you only the way you allow them to.

THE RIGHT FRIENDS

The wonderful benefit of having lived in five different countries is that I have been blessed with such a rich variety of friends. Some friends have stayed friends over long periods of time, without much contact, while others haven't. Some I feel I can call any time –

some I don't. Some friends are very different from me, while other are very similar. With some I share similar hobbies and interests, whereas with others I don't. No matter what the situation is now, I am so grateful for having met every single one of them.

I don't really like phone calls and long phone calls are even worse. Now add four children into that equation and you can see how difficult phone calls to friends can be. Especially a meaningful conversation. I prefer to meet them in person and have a chat, but even this is a challenge in respect of my time. Social media helps, of course, and WhatsApp messages are also a great tool. For me, a friendship is a great one when there is no pressure from either side. We may not see each other for a long time, but when we do, it's like seeing each other yesterday. I personally think we don't have to be in contact constantly. Yes, at the beginning of a friendship there is that getting-to-know-one-another phase and that may require more time together to establish the friendship. But once the friendship is there, one of the best feelings in the world is knowing that it is so special that I can call at any time, drop by and without having spoken in ages we can take up where we left off last time, even if last time was a month or more ago.

My friends are similar to me and also very different. What is important is that there is trust and a mutual understanding of what friendship is. As with all relationships, there needs to be some common ground. That does not mean we have to have similar jobs or hobbies. We don't need to have the same taste in clothes or mutual friends or even the same travel destinations. In fact, I'm often more energised and have super interesting conversations with my friends who are totally different from me.

I've noticed that my friends and I often start out sharing a common interest and then life happens, and we move off in totally different directions. I met friends at my fashion design courses; some were younger, some older, but at the time we had similar interests. Now we live on different continents and have different jobs (not all fashion-related). Some of us have families and some don't. The amazing thing about friendship is that some of us have stayed friends over the years and over the changes that we have been through. A few have moved on and we are no longer friends, but that's OK; life changes, we move on, it is normal.

For example,when an old friend and colleague whom I hadn't seen in 10 years called me and asked to meet up for coffee during his visit to Dubai and we did, everything was still the same. As if we saw each other just a few weeks ago. Ten years − can you imagine? Obviously, we did not have enough time to catch up on everything, but overall, the friendship was still the same.

A similar story that reminds me of this special bond is that of speaking to a friend about her dream of starting a new business. Although so much had happened since we had last spoken, the old connection was there instantly. When my friends who used to live in Dubai come and visit, it's as though we just saw each other yesterday. That's what a great friendship is for me.

Remember Lisa, the friend I mentioned that I met online? We have never met in person, but we regularly Zoom call or Skype chat. Although we have not met, we are always there for each other. Even that is possible in this new world and with the internet. It's a different kind of friendship. I don't really know her kids or husband or family; we have connected on another level and I don't know what it would be like if we were neighbours, but I do know that I trust her completely and we are totally honest with each other. That is what counts for me. Thank you, Lisa, for being the kind of friend who makes me a better person and for supporting me to write this book.

Of course, there are friends I used to have and our lives have taken us in different directions. With a few, it was the fact that I got married and had kids and they were still single, or I moved countries and we just did not stay in contact. It's not that anything happened between us; we merely lost contact, as so often happens when moving far away. I am very lucky that I still have a few very old friends, some going back to when I was three years old. We grew up together, we went to school together and were very close. But some of them are completely different now. I'm forever grateful for these friendships. We know each other like sisters and the feeling of having them there for me when I need them and vice versa is priceless. We haven't lived in the same city for a long time, and I don't share the same hobbies with some of them anymore, but there is a deeper connection that will not go away and I love seeing how everyone has developed.

With my kids growing up in Dubai, in a largely expat community, where people come and go all the time, I just hope that some of their childhood friendships will remain as strong as mine and last for a lifetime, as mine hopefully will. I will do whatever I can to support them and let them visit each other, even if they don't live in the same country anymore. By writing this down here, you can hold me accountable.

SURROUND YOURSELF WITH POSITIVE PEOPLE

I once read somewhere that your relationships are like elevators: they either lift you up or they bring you down. For me and my life, I want friends who lift me up rather than push me down. I am a positive person and I choose to be surrounded by positive people.

Only you can decide who you want to be surrounded by and only you can define what a great friendship looks like. Maybe you need to talk every day. Maybe you don't. The important value of friendship is that your friends are there for you, in the same way that you are there for them when one of you is in need. Are your friendships fuelling you? Do they lift you up? Do your friends give without wanting something in return? Do they listen to what you have to say? Are they honest? Is it a give and take? Are you feeling judged? Are you judging them? These are some of the questions you can ask yourself to establish what a good friendship means for you.

What you don't have to do is be friends with someone because it is expected of you or because they are part of your group of friends or because of group pressure. I think it is possible to be friendly with someone without actually being friends. When you meet someone, they don't have to be your friend if they don't meet your values for friendship. This is the time when you choose to just be friendly.

Let's talk about group pressure and friendship. I have seen groups of friends where there is such pressure to do everything together. Everyone needs to be invited to every dinner, cafe and playdate. I have planned parties before and thought to myself, "If I invite this person, I should invite that person." I have heard this numerous times from friends as well. Why do women do this? I am specifically saying women here because I honestly don't know a single man who thinks this way. I mean, you are an adult; you should be able to stand up for your own beliefs. Look at children and copy them; if my son does not want to invite someone to his party, he doesn't, and there is no way I can change his mind just because I may be friends with the mother. It is his party and he chooses. Don't allow yourself to be pressured by a group. I get that you don't want to hurt anybody, but if you are not really friends with someone why do you need to invite them?

I decided a long time ago that I would not go down that route anymore. It is my life, my house, my party, my decision. If I don't want to spend time with someone, I won't. However, if you choose to do this, you should remember that it works both ways. You can't be disappointed when you are suddenly the one who is not invited. I know it's hard. But I assure you, once you know who your true friends are, once others know what you stand for, this will rarely happen.

What is always true is that a friend and anybody you spend more time with should be positive. Look for people who lift you up rather than push you down. Look for people who want the best for you rather than only think about themselves. I would also say, look for people who are not judgmental. I have listened to other people so much that I adapted a lot to the friends and family I surrounded myself with, often not in a positive way. I am not proud of excluding my friend at university and would rather forget about it, but it is also a good reminder that I should surround myself with positive people.

FAMILY

Although not the same as friends, I would say this applies to family as well. I would never suggest that you walk away and never see your family. I truly believe that blood is thicker than anything: it ties us together. Family members are the ones that should be there for each other, regardless of what has happened in the past. However, if a family member is so toxic and is affecting you too much, I do say don't spend too much time together. You do not have to celebrate every holiday with your family members.

My friend Maria has to go to her husband's family every Christmas for a week. Her husband turns into a little boy again; every wish is his mother's command and my friend is totally ignored. She has endured this for many years and her marriage has suffered. We have talked about it many times and I kept saying that she needs to find a compromise. As we live abroad, it can be a challenge. We can't just see our family for a few hours and leave again. It is usually at least a week and we stay in one house together. However, there are always solutions. In my friend's situation, this could be renting an Airbnb flat so that everyone still has some privacy. They could take turns and spend one year with the parents-in-law and one year without. They could invite them to Dubai for Christmas (where at least they would be in her house). They could say they won't come home for Christmas, but spend a week during a different holiday together – one that she can organise in a neutral place away from both their homes. There are many different options that would allow her to set her boundaries, without neglecting her parents-in-law.

The thing is that you have to sit down and discuss this with your partner and find options that work for both. At the end of the day, it is your life, your partnership and not theirs. If they don't want to discuss this difficult topic or they ignore the problem, (I know that feeling very well and I know how frustrating it can be) remember that you always have a choice. You can think of different options yourself and present them to your partner. I know from my experience with Gordon that he just does not want to think about it, but once I sat him down and explained how I felt and presented him with options that would work for me, he listened. By presenting him with options, he can still choose, and he has the feeling of being in charge. Nobody likes a partner who just complains or holds a gun to their heads with an ultimatum. This would make the situation very reactive and not helpful at all. Yes, the solution may be harmful for a family member. But if it is communicated in the right way, it is at the end of the day everyone's choice how to react and how to deal with a situation. You are responsible for your life and not theirs. They are not responsible for your life. If it works both ways, and if everyone is supporting the other family members it is perfect, but it has to be a give and take situation.

Family is very important to me and I can't imagine a life where I don't have a relationship with my kids or am not as close to them as we are now. But I am also a realist and it would depend on life's circumstances, or the kind of partners and friends my kids choose to surround themselves with in the future. It is clearly my big wish that we always come together as a big family and have long family dinners around a massive table. I know that this may not happen, and I will not push my kids. It needs to be their choice; all I can do is offer the possibility to them. I want my kids to feel the same way; they must want to spend that time with us. I want my kids to know that they don't need to obey their parents' wishes just because we wish it. There is always a solution and choice.

HOW TO FIND THE RIGHT PEOPLE

You may be asking yourself now how you can actually change your existing surroundings. There are people in your life – your family, your work colleagues and friends – who have been there for years, and if you are in school or university, obviously your classmates. I get it; there are people you can't just get rid of or not see anymore. True, but as I said before, you can find a compromise that works for everyone and of course you can choose your future. You can choose to spend more time with the right people in your spare time and you can prepare for the future. I also believe you can have different friends for different occasions. I have never had just one best friend; I have always had friends who I like to travel with more than others, or friends who I love to go shopping with. I have friends who I would call when I have to make a difficult decision, and friends who I love to sit with for hours and just talk. It does not mean that one friend is better than the other.

I thought it would help if I write down how and where I find friends, as I often get asked this question or run into it in our groups.

Most importantly, you can find the right people through a joint hobby, interest or goal.

My hobbies are usually sport-related and, in my experience, sporty people are usually fun, fair and open. They make good friends and as you share a common hobby or goal, you'll definitely have something to talk about.

I am sure this is just as true when you share a common interest in music or books. You can join a book club, for example, or there may be something like a music club. Other places where you can meet friends are conferences, meet-ups and online groups around a joint topic of interest.

What I have found is that it is always good to talk about your interests and what you are looking for. Once I started talking about my interest in yoga and meditation, I suddenly met so many people who were yoga teachers and had classes. As a result, I have great new connections and conversations that I never thought would happen.

Another example of being open was when I was seeking a mastermind group, a group of businesswomen to meet regularly to support and hold each other accountable. I was looking, but didn't really share that with anyone. One day, I started talking about it to a few people at a networking event. The outcome was that I met someone that evening who was looking for something similar and we decided to start it together. A few weeks later, we met for the first time with four other business owners. It has been an amazing journey and I now have five fabulous women who I feel I can totally rely on and whom I would never have met had I not opened up and shared my idea.

These days, with the internet, it is quite easy to meet people, online and offline. You can look at the meetup.com website, for example, and see what kind of meetups are being organised in your area. My friend and Mums in Biz podcast co-host Kyla started a meetup a few years ago for mums who had children at home, but still wanted to go networking. She looked for a child-friendly cafe and put it on meetup.com. That's how I met her. I wanted to go out, network and talk about business instead of breastfeeding and nappies for the fourth time in my life. So I went. It was great; I spent time with my baby and had such inspiring and uplifting conversations. Of course, I also met Kyla and the ultimate outcome was the podcast that we started together, which I love.

Kyla told me a story about one lady who said she would also come to her networking morning. However, when she arrived and saw us sitting inside the cafe through the window, we all looked like we were close friends to her and her confidence left her. She turned around and went home. We had all met about 10 minutes earlier. But we had a common interest, mums who ran their own business.

It happens: you decide to go somewhere new and there are people who know each other already. Don't let that stop you. If you don't try to meet them, you will never find out whether there was a good friend to be made or a special connection among those people. Having moved abroad, without the comforting surroundings of a workplace and colleagues who were immediately there for me, I was often forced to go to events, gatherings and meetups alone. They were not always successful and sometimes quite simply horrible. Not everyone is as welcoming or not every group and person is for you. But you need to give it a try.

I clearly remember a German mums' group in America. I was a new mum with a baby who cried a lot. I was still relatively new in the city, so I took the opportunity of having a baby to go and meet other mums. By the way, babies, toddlers and dogs make it very easy to meet like-minded people. I have met many great friends through my kids or just by standing on a playground. But of course, you have to start a conversation.

Anyway, going back to that German mums' group. It took me about an hour to get there; it was quite far, and I got lost. Once I arrived, nobody really greeted me. They all knew each other already and, worse, my son started crying almost right from the start. I tried to feed him, but it did not really help. After trying to calm him in another room and trying to start a conversation with some of the mums who looked kind of open and friendly, I left exhausted and upset. Nobody had made the effort to engage with me.

None of the other mums reacted to me trying to start a conversation despite my screaming son. None of them tried to help in any way, and the description of a nice, friendly mums' group (I can't remember where I found it) was definitely not what I experienced that day. Honestly, it was a devastating experience and I was so glad to leave. I drove back with silent tears running down my face and my son sleeping happily in his car seat. Back then, I swore I would never go to a German mums' group again. Well, that was not the right choice, of course. But you know what I mean. At least I knew I had tried. I had given it a chance. I tried different mums' groups and found many wonderful mothers and one truly great friend among them, whom I still miss dearly after moving away.

It takes a little bit of time, effort and disappointment, but I assure you once you start you will meet great friends. You just need to be open. Oh, and by the way, if you go somewhere to meet people – take it from someone who is not an introvert, but who has been very shy – you don't necessarily need to be the one who approaches everyone, but you need to *look* open. Smile at people, don't cross your arms in front of your body (it looks like you are protecting yourself against some kind of danger), greet everyone, say something even if it is just about the weather. You will see, the right people will find you.

It may be a huge step outside your comfort zone, but to be open to new possibilities you need to start somewhere. Take the opportunity of practising every time you go somewhere – say a little more, smile at a few more people. I never used to talk to the people at the supermarket checkout, but decided to use this as an opportunity to practise, so one day I started by smiling at them. The next time I said a few words (probably about the weather) and then I wished them a good day before I left.

When I lived in Texas I was taken aback, especially in the beginning, by how people would just randomly comment or start conversations with each other. This seemed almost alien to me, as a reserved German (now there's a judgmental statement for you), and now I love it. I have had some great conversations with total strangers since I lived there.

My friend Kyla is an expert at this. We travelled together from Dubai to New York and then on to Minnesota, and she loves talking to anybody, anywhere. Sometimes a little more than needed. She would start conversations at flight check-ins, hotel check-ins, restaurants, cafes and anywhere where there was an opportunity. She told me, while recording a podcast, that it is her self-assigned task at the moment to find out a bit more about the lady who works at the local coffee shop where she goes every morning before work. It may sound easy, but I challenge you to give it a try to find out for yourself and to train yourself. I'm sure it will be a lovely experience.

There was a time when I said, "Good morning!" to everyone I met during the day. If I was on my bike cycling to school with my kids, I would greet every person that came walking, jogging or cycling past. Yes, it took me outside my comfort zone, but I got some great responses and I got better at it over time. It was a very nice start to the day.

I promise you, give it a try. Start by practising in small ways, as I did, and very soon you will be able to start a conversation with anyone. I have experienced it at first hand. You just need to give it a chance.

I HAVE LEARNED THAT I HAVE A CHOICE ABOUT WHOM I SURROUND MYSELF WITH:

1. I choose to be around positive people, people who lift me up.

2. If something or someone doesn't feel right, I can walk away. There is always a way.

3. There are many different ways of finding the right people; I just have to go and look for them.

4. I have the choice to let go of people if they are toxic.

5. The right friends will be there for me, no matter what.

CHAPTER SEVEN

LOOK FOR THE POSITIVE

As I started writing this chapter the news came through that schools would remain closed and we would continue homeschooling until the end of the school year in Dubai. We had the kids home for over three weeks at this point and then they extended it to another three months. Followed by the usual two months of summer holiday.

I honestly just had to laugh. It was so ironic that while sitting here writing about looking for the positive in any situation, I was struggling to find the time to even write this book, manage all four of my kids with their homeschooling and working for my business. Instead the house was a mess, there was someone in every room, there were constant questions and I didn't have an office anymore so I couldn't close the door and shut out the noise. I was worried about the world and what was going on in it. I was worried I wouldn't be able to see my family in Germany any time soon and

I missed my time alone, my sport outside (we were almost on full lockdown) and honestly I missed the few quiet hours at home when the kids were at school and Gordon was at work. The truth is that I was struggling just like many other mums I know.

This gave me the perfect opportunity to practise what I preach… I didn't let negative thoughts take over my life. Yes, I have them too, but I know a brain can't process both the negatives and the positives. I choose to think of the positives. I sat down and thought about all the positives of this situation; I told myself to dig deeper. Yes, I enjoyed having this family time and the kids were happy to be around us so much more, but surely I could find more. There must be other reasons that are positive, that will remain with us. And immediately the song *Always Look on the Bright Side of Life* popped into my head. I hadn't listened to that song in years and I don't know where it came from but now I couldn't stop humming it and it made me smile. I looked up the lyrics and it actually speaks the truth for me; we have to keep on laughing and whistling, life might seem very hard sometimes, but when we look at the good things, the little things and keep smiling, life will be so much easier and we will spread this feeling of happiness to others.

We all have to remember that there is something good in everything. There is a solution to every problem.

And you can change how you look at things, how you see the world. I once heard that when you feel stuck you are essentially choosing not to change perspective. I feel that this is so true. You can choose to look at a situation from a different angle and find the positives or find a solution.

For me, in this situation, it was finding out more about my kids' schooling, what and how they learn. We had fun recording videos and I watched them make small films, which was amazing. It was a great time for all six of us to connect with each other. In addition, I found that doing homeschooling somehow brought me a lot of joy. It wasn't what I dreamed of doing and I won't choose to do it again, but for the time being, it was fun. Together we learned about plastic in the oceans and greenhouse gases, we learned long division with the help of YouTube, and we laughed at my pronunciation of Arabic words. I found out that I'm capable of things that I would never have known, had it not been for this unique situation. Having the kids at home 24/7 is something I would have dreaded, yet now that I was doing it and had no choice, it worked. And I was a lot calmer than I thought I would be.

In addition, the kids helped with cooking and learned a lot around the kitchen. They saw me exercising, working on my business and writing this book. The things I usually do alone. They became curious and even joined in. Felicia decided she would write her own book, which I thought was great.

IS YOUR GLASS HALF EMPTY OR HALF FULL?

Even though I always knew inside me that I was strong and could figure anything out, I used to be the kind of person who said, "The problem is..." – I saw the negative in situations. Now this is a sentence I have cut out of my vocabulary. I have learned to look for the positive. And so can you.

I decided that for my life, my glass would always be half full, which means that there is a chance in every situation. There will always be problems in life, hurdles we have to overcome. If you change your mindset and see them as opportunities, your life will become a lot more fun and enjoyable.

Again the situation with Covid-19 was the best example of that conscious decision. Dubai was one of the first cities to react quite drastically to the situation. And now it was up to us, the citizens to make the choice to see this as our glass being half empty or half full. It was our choice to either drown in worry, anxiety or even self pity or to pull ourselves together, stand up and make the best of it.

As a family, we made the latter choice. We adapted every week and we got better at creating a new daily routine. We changed our way of living, our way of thinking and looked for joy together every single day. I have to admit, I struggled when so many people were losing their jobs, knowing that so many people had it far worse than we did. But I realised it would not help anybody if I sat at home being worried about the world. So I concentrated on what I could do, I supported the people I could support. I reminded myself that every little action helps.

As I sit here writing this piece at 5.30am, I can hear the birds chirping outside. I am grateful for how lucky we are. I am reminded that there were many nights when the kids went to bed and they would tell me that they had a great day. This was also a time for Gordon and myself, we knew that we get along better when we spend more time together.

This was true for our family, and I saw it in so many others too. There was so much bonding going on in so many families, which was amazing to see. Even though I would never have chosen this scenario, this new life has made us stronger as a family and we have become even closer. Extreme situations have a way of embedding themselves in our memories, and I hope that the good memories of this situation will outweigh the bad ones. I wonder how much of this we will remember.

It was great to see so many people finding new solutions to be active. Running inside a flat, running inside the garage and of course running in the garden. I read of people who ran marathons at home, even triathlons and a Full Ironman. One guy here in Dubai even ran 100km in his garden. I'm grateful that we have a garden and that the weather wasn't so hot yet. I started running in the garden and I managed 8km by running loops of 40m, which I never thought would be possible.

Remember there is a solution and chance in every situation. You just have to look for it and figure it out. You can choose to have a glass that is half full.

THERE IS A POSITIVE IN EVERY SITUATION

I'm sure you have heard the saying, or someone has even said it to you, "There is something positive in every situation." I have, many times, and for a long time found this hard to believe. I immediately thought of losing a job, illness, death and big natural disasters. When I think back on my life now, it is true. There was a positive in every situation – I just had to look for it; sometimes it was easy to see and sometimes I had to REALLY look for it.

When Gordon and I got married, we'd planned for much of the wedding reception to be outside. We rented a beautiful house with an even more beautiful garden, especially for the reception. It was the middle of the summer in Germany and although we had planned for some rain, we had not planned for non-stop, 24-hour rain. It started the night before and didn't stop until late into the night of our wedding day. The house was too small for all the people and it was super tight in there. Many people got wet waiting to get into the house, and if that was not enough of a disaster, a friend had to be rushed to hospital after choking on his food. The rain and this incident were all everyone talked about. It felt as if everyone would remember only the disasters.

As well as Gordon and I getting married that day, another very special and unexpected situation happened because of the rain. After the choking incident, one of my best friends suddenly found herself seated next to my cousin. They fell in love that rainy day and are now married and have three beautiful children themselves. Looking for the positive here is not difficult. And everyone remembers our wedding very clearly, even if it was only for the volume of rain that fell from the sky that day. People remember extreme situations.

None of my first three pregnancies were particularly easy or enjoyable, but apart from the obvious, having three healthy wonderful kids, I do see other positives in them now.

Around the time I became pregnant with my first son, I was also diagnosed with precancerous cells in my cervix. I had been tested two months before and everything was fine, so I was totally shocked by that diagnosis, as it was a drastic new development. I had gone to the gynaecologist in the US because I had heard that it was easier to be accepted once you were pregnant if you had been a patient there before, and because becoming pregnant seemed to take longer than expected.

I'm a doer and a fixer. Once I decide on something, I get it done, so I was expecting that once I decided to have kids I would get pregnant right there and then. But instead of getting tips on how to become pregnant, I was told something did not look normal, I needed further testing. It felt as though she had pushed me miles back from what I wanted, rather than helping me achieve it.

The biopsy itself was one of the most painful things I have experienced in my life and the result was crushing. I remember that the day I got the result and the nurse told me I needed surgery to remove the bad cells was the same day I did my first pregnancy test in my life. It was positive and I was in tears on the bathroom floor. What should have been amazing news came with some of the worst news I had experienced in my otherwise healthy life.

To cut a long story short, I picked myself up, found another doctor as well as a specialist in cervical cancer. We lived in Houston, Texas, which at the time was one of the best cancer research cities in the world. I was closely monitored during my pregnancy, gave birth to my son, and two months later I had surgery, which went very well.

To be honest, this pregnancy was not easy. There were a lot of worries. I knew that apart from a baby growing in my belly there was also something else that was unfathomable developing in my body. Besides that, I had smaller issues, such as not being able to walk properly, feeling nauseous all the time and regular nose bleeds. I wondered who would actually like pregnancy. Looking back at the situation now, I know I came out of it so much stronger. And I am so grateful to my close friend Teresa in Houston, who supported me hugely during that time. I met amazing doctors, and since then have been a lot more grateful for my health. I also know I can get through a situation like this physically and mentally. During my subsequent pregnancies, I was monitored more closely, which made me feel quite good and safe.

Being me, I thought the next pregnancy would only be better. And because we didn't know what the future might bring, we decided to just let it be and quite quickly I became pregnant for the second time. My two sons are only 17 months apart, which I think is amazing.

Whereas the first pregnancy was hard because of the uncertainty, the second one proved to be a lot harder physically. At 20 weeks, on Maximilian's first birthday, I developed a strange stomach ache that I knew felt different. I called my doctor and went for a check-up. I was told I was having contractions, only halfway through my pregnancy. He sent me over to the hospital right away and within a few hours from the pain starting, I was lying in a hospital bed flat on my back – on my son's first birthday. I was in tears. For the rest of my pregnancy, I had to learn to rest and slow down. I spent a lot of time lying; everything I did was very careful, and I had to take medication to prevent contractions a few times. I had to go to hospital one more time, but eventually I learned to listen to my body very closely and was able to avoid another hospital visit.

But it got worse. The constant lying in bed, coupled with the back problems that I had suffered before, which I basically ignored until it was too late, meant that I was now not sleeping at all. I was in too much pain. I was diagnosed as having a slipped disc and even though I was so against it, I took very strong medication. I was supposed to rest as much as possible, but I now urgently also had to do exercises to strengthen my back. To be honest, it was a very hard time, not only physically, as I had a toddler to look after as well, but also mentally. I had to stay positive and not stress myself, to stay calm for my baby and avoid new contractions.

Luckily Nicholas stayed put until the end and arrived only two days early. I was able to heal my back through lots of exercises after his birth, something that I do to this day.

There were many positives I took out of these painful and worrying months. Gordon and I became very close during that tough time; we were far away from family and had little help, but together we got through this and I think it helped establish a bond that nobody can take away from us. I am grateful that I lived in Houston, THE medical city, during those times, and that I had an amazing doctor who was there for me through both of those pregnancies. I could trust him one thousand percent and both Gordon and I will never forget him. I am grateful for the very supportive friends I had during that time, including my amazing friend Jule, who came all the way from Canada to stay with me and help me when Gordon had to travel for a week.

Something that will also stay with me for the rest of my life is that I really got to know my body. I learned to feel when something was not right and I learned to really care for my back and take care of my body. I guess I had taken it for granted, which is probably normal when you are young. During those two pregnancies, I learned that I have to take care of this body if I wanted it to support me in my goal of reaching the age of 100 years.

One memory that will last forever from this period of time is of doing water exercises – which I had been told to do for my back to recover – with a bunch of grandmas and granddads, who were so friendly and truly happy to have a young lady with them in the pool. They treated me like a queen. I am smiling while writing this, thinking of this group whose names I don't know, but whose faces I can still see and whose voices I can still hear. I assume that some of them may not be with us anymore. They didn't know it, but they left a profound impression on me.

My lesson from that was that we will always leave a footprint and a legacy somewhere, even if we don't know about it.

When something happens to someone close to you, it may be easier for you to see the positives, rather than the person in the middle of it. Not too long ago, while living in Dubai, Gordon lost his job. His job is the reason we are here. If you want to live in Dubai, you need to have a job which provides a visa and health insurance, usually for the whole family. If you lose it, you have a one-month grace period in which to get a new visa and find a new job. When Gordon was made redundant, it happened quite out of the blue. At least for him; although he knew it might be a possibility, he did not really believe that it would happen. He was not prepared, mentally, for the shock of losing his job and having to look for a new one. Basically, he did not see it coming and was thrown in at the deep end. Something he had not experienced before. The pressure of feeling responsible for a family of six weighed heavily on his shoulders. We knew we could get visas through my company, but obviously that plus health insurance would be a huge cost factor. In addition, he was so disappointed in his old boss, whom he had considered a friend, that it was almost paralysing for him. His first instinct was to blame everyone else and feel sorry for himself. It was just not fair.

He did not see it at the time, but as I was only indirectly affected, I saw all the positives in the situation. First and foremost, he began to be interested in personal development; he started reading books about it and he hired a coach. Growth and development, which I was so interested in and could never really talk to him about, were suddenly topics we talked about almost every evening. Although not all of it stayed with him when he found a new job, I can see he is more aware. He has continued seeing a coach and is taking online classes with me. He even agreed to come with me to a personal development conference. In addition, we talked a lot about where we wanted to live, what the future should look like and whether it was time to leave. And of course, he gained a lot of experience being interviewed, he met new people and if this were to happen again we would both be more prepared financially.

You would have to talk to him about it in more detail, but he has also learned a lot about who his real friends are, and about his strengths and weaknesses.

LIFE IS NOT UNFAIR

"Life is not unfair. Life is what you make of it."

Hrithik Roshan

When I said to my son one day that life is just not fair and we have to accept it, I could hear myself saying it as though I were someone else listening, and I was shocked about my own words. It really got me thinking. I learned this phrase when I grew up. I had heard it a thousand times and it was sort of engrained in me. Saying it out loud to my son, teaching him this phrase, I caught myself and started to ask, "Is that really true?"

I don't think this way anymore. I haven't for some time. In fact, trying to remember a time when I believed this is difficult. Nothing comes to mind. I believe that everything happens for a reason and that, depending on your perspective of life, you can choose to see any situation as a negative or a positive.

I think back to all the times I struggled with things in my life and thought it was so unfair that *everybody* else was so confident and I wasn't and on top of it *everybody* had an amazing body. I felt uncomfortable in mine. I think back to how I believed that *every girl* I knew had a boyfriend and I didn't. Once I had a boyfriend who dumped me for another girl and *nobody* else had been dumped, just me. I think back to how I felt *everybody* had got a good grade and I didn't, despite my working the hardest for it; that *everybody* in class could remember the poem for language arts and I just could not; that *everybody* earned more money than I, but I was the one staying in the office the latest; that *everybody's* businesses were thriving and mine wasn't even though I worked so hard; that *everybody* was a fast runner and I just could not get any faster – and the list goes on. Was it really *everybody* or *nobody*? No, it wasn't. It just seemed that way to me at the time.

Now, I can think of all the positives in my life and for each of those situations I mentioned above I can find the positive by changing my perspective. Yes, for other people confidence came easily but they didn't have the chance to teach other people how to become confident, as they had never experienced being shy. Yes, many girls in my class had the 'better' looking bodies, curvier or bustier bodies, but I have never struggled with weight issues in my life. I am over 40 now and hardly anybody would guess that. This body has carried four babies, given birth four times and breastfed for many years, when so many other women I know struggle to even conceive. How can I think it is unfair that my body does not have the perfect proportions?

When I asked Maximilian the other day what he thinks is unfair in life, he thought a little bit and then responded that poor people becoming even poorer and rich people becoming even richer was unfair. I asked him whether that was always the case. We then went on to talk about whether rich people are happier in their lives just because they have money. I asked him, "What about the people we met in Ethiopia who had almost nothing, but were singing and laughing so much? Did they seem unhappy? What about the amazing countryside they lived in? They didn't seem to think that their life was unfair. They actually seemed very happy." He thought for a while, and we agreed together that fairness and happiness does not depend on money. It depends on so many things, some of which are covered in this book. But the statement that life in general is not fair is debatable.

I, myself, came to the conclusion that, despite what I thought many times throughout my life, despite having to work harder than others for many things, I was blessed with a great start in life and now it was my duty to make something out of it. I can't waste this opportunity, the one opportunity I have in life.

Now I help my kids to look at their problems from a different perspective. Sometimes they get it and sometimes they don't. Often, we all end up laughing. I know they will learn to question beliefs for their life and to look at things from a different perspective, and hopefully this will make them happier than I was for a long time.

Give it a try and question yourself. When you catch yourself thinking something is unfair, that life is hard, ask yourself, "Why is it unfair? Is it really that hard, that unfair, in the grand scheme of things? What is the positive that you can see right now? What happened to me before the situation became unfair? How can I see the situation from a different perspective? In a different light?"

BEING GRATEFUL

"You have to live through the worst of life, so you never take the best parts for granted."

Unknown

A word that did not exist in my vocabulary for a long time was 'gratefulness'. When we moved to America, I learned about Thanksgiving, which we had never celebrated in my home before. We did not really grow up with the concept of giving thanks. I did hear my mum say she was so grateful for her healthy children and sometimes we prayed before dinner and gave thanks, but I guess it never really stayed with me.

It really hit me when I had kids. Without realising it at first, I started being grateful for so many things in my life. It started with the big things like holding a healthy baby in my arms and I went on to appreciate the small things, such as my son walking in the park and being so happy about every 'amu' (ant) he found on the way. I am a person who is constantly doing things, always busy; I can't sit still, but I learned from my kids to pause and appreciate them. To pause and be grateful.

A few years ago, I started being more conscious about it. At first, I began to think about what I was grateful for in my life, every day, and after a while I started writing it down every morning. I write down very small things, for example, how sweet Felicia looks with her skiing hat and pyjamas; how Lavinia sings every day on the way home from school; how the sun is shining; how cold it still is in Dubai although it usually is much warmer this time of year; about the water in the shower still being cold (it gets very hot during the summer months); how we all laughed out loud together at a joke Gordon made; about how my hair looks today; how my friend recommended a good book to me today. You get it – the things are not always the big things, such as my health; they can be very small things, such as a hot coffee in the morning. Something that made me happy.

What that does is it makes me look for the good things throughout the day; it makes me pause for a second and appreciate the small things. Because I now notice these things, I focus on them and the positives become bigger and more numerous. It ultimately makes me a happier person. Plus, it is addictive and contagious. Once you start a practice like this, and start talking about it and sharing, other people will start. Your immediate family may start; more people are happier, and that makes the world a happier place. One person at a time.

I spoke about that in my speech at my 40th birthday party. One of my friends came up to me afterwards and thanked me for mentioning that I take the time to pause to appreciate Lavinia looking so happily at a butterfly. It took me a long time to not be impatient in those moments when there are so many other things that need to be done, and now it makes me see the beauty of this butterfly as well. It makes me appreciate the seemingly small things in our lives. She sent me a text message a few weeks later, saying that she had been out with her kids the other day and instead of being annoyed that they slowed her down by looking at every bug and thinking about the dinner that had to be made, she paused and really appreciated the moment with her kids. I don't think I will ever forget that text message. It made me so happy.

If the only thing reading this book achieves is to make you pause and appreciate something small today, something that will make you smile, and you will then try again tomorrow, it was worth writing. Look for the little things. There are numerous little but positive things out there that make your life better. As I wrote before, your brain is wired in such a way that you can't think of the positive and the negative at the same time. If you choose to think about positive things, even if they are insignificant, you will generally be a lot happier and more positive. And that will make the whole world a better place.

Hopefully, mine today is making you appreciate those small things in your life.

At the end of this book there is a page for you to start writing down the things you are grateful for in your life today. You can then continue by writing one more thing down every day, this can be in this book, on a piece of paper, in your phone or anywhere, it is just important that you do it. Once you get into the habit more, you can increase the number of things you write.

I HAVE LEARNED THAT I HAVE THE CHOICE TO LOOK FOR THE POSITIVE:

1. In every situation there is something positive, even if it is visible only much later.

2. There are no problems, just possibilities and the glass is always half full, not half empty.

3. What I see is what I focus on. I choose to see the positives.

4. Practising gratitude will make me look for the small positive things that are around me every single day.

5. Looking for the positives makes me a happier human being and it makes the world a happier place.

CHAPTER EIGHT

SOMEDAY IS A MYTH

We have all said something along the lines of, "I'll do that *once* I am grown up," or "I'll start *once* I have more time," or "I'll do that *once* I have the money," or "I'll start to do that again *once* I have lost my extra weight."

What if that *once* never happens? What if you never have enough time or money? What if you never lose the weight? Or what if you die before you have the time?

We got the sad news that a colleague of my husband had died at the age of 68. He was due to retire this summer. Maybe he had plans that he wanted to do once he retired. Maybe he never got to travel to that country that he always wanted to go to. I don't know. The one thing I do know is that I never want to look back one day and say I wished I had done this or that, but never did.

There are always reasons why you can't do things. I know. I am very good at telling myself why I can't do things. I have been wanting to write this book for a few years now; I started writing a few times and have stopped multiple times. Something always got in the way – either my work, or my kids, or my sport. Or my ego telling me that the idea was absolute nonsense: nobody would want to read what I write. I told myself that once I had more time, once I had more knowledge about self-development, once my kids were older and would actually read the book, I would write it.

I'll be honest; it was not easy, but one of my strengths is following through and acting, so I told those voices to stop, to go away. One reason why I wanted to write this book was that if something happened to me, my words would be on paper for my children. And I always knew I wanted to dedicate one whole chapter to this myth of 'someday'. What example was I setting by not writing this book? It was not like me to postpone this book, or any other goal, every single day for years.

I decided to act and hired a book coach to hold me accountable and to push me to do what I wanted to do. And oh man, I am so happy I did it, because I can tell you I would have never written this book during coronavirus times with my kids at home if I had done it alone.

YOU ARE NEVER READY

I was not ready to write this book. I am not an author; I had no clue how to go about writing and publishing a book. English is my second language. This is developing into a self-help book, and I am not a psychologist or anything like that.

When Kyla and I decided to start our podcast together, I was not ready. In fact, I didn't know anything about recording podcasts or editing. When I decided I would be a website designer, I had only ever designed two websites, one of them my own. When I signed up for my first half-marathon or my first Half Ironman, I was not ready: I still had lots of training to do. When I had my first son, I did not realise what I was getting into; I did not grasp the magnitude of what I was letting myself in for, with motherhood – for life!

I knew all of that and I did it anyway. I learned on the job, I started, I practised and I got better. But the first step was to start, and not wait for a better time or what I thought would be a better time.

If you are reading this and you are a mum, you were probably not ready either when you had your baby. Did you know what was coming exactly? Why are you even hesitating one second with things like starting a business, signing up for a marathon, travelling to Europe for the first time or going to a spinning class? You have a child; a child is for life and you are managing all right. Nothing that I have written here is for life. I mean it can be, but it doesn't have to be. You can always stop and there won't be any implications. You can't stop being a mum. So, tell me again, why are you not ready?

And if you are not a mum, because you think you are not ready, let me tell you: you will never be ready! I have four kids and I was not ready to have a first, a second, a third or a fourth. I did not know what exactly was coming, I did not know how I would manage; I did not know whether they would be healthy. I didn't know much. But I figured it out. My body figured it out. And so will you. Millions of other women have and so can you. And by the way, in case nobody else has ever said it to you, being a mum is the most wonderful thing in life and you will not really understand this until you become a mum. You don't understand what real, unconditional love means until you have a child. You don't know what you as a person are capable of until you have a baby and have to step up for your child.

If you are younger or don't have kids yet, my advice is simply to do as much as you can now. Travel the world, work for that NGO, work your way up the career ladder, start your own business, run that first half-marathon – whatever it is that you want to do someday, do it now. You will not be any more or any less ready for this or for a baby later in life. Take it from a mum: following your dreams and anything else you want to achieve in life is a little bit more difficult when you have kids. I am doing it, but I wish I had done more before I became a mum. At the same time, having children will make life a lot more worth living, so don't postpone that either.

If you are a man reading this, my advice is the same. There is no difference between a mother and a father. Apart from the fact that women give birth. I am sure that watching your beloved partner squeezing a human out of her body and being in such pain is potentially even harder than doing it yourself. For me, at least, I prefer to do the really hard things myself instead of watching someone I love having to go through them. So, hats off to you! I feel this needs to be said as well. And for the women here, feel free to pass this on to your partner, brother or father.

THERE IS NEVER THE RIGHT TIME

No there is not. But you still need to start. Let me give it to you straight up: the right time will probably not come. And if it does, you can still start now; you will have an advantage once the right time comes.

Having spoken to so many women who want to start their own business, I have heard so many reasons why they can't yet. Of course, the most common reason is, "There is not enough time." Other reasons include not having the right or enough knowledge, not having enough money, not being able to leave a job just yet, needing to learn more, someone else doing it already and the list goes on. And guess what, yes, some of it may be true, and still the time will not be right. There will always be something that comes up and there will always be an excuse in the way. I know, I have told myself so many times throughout my life why I can't do things.

The truth is that these are just excuses. It's that inner voice, the one that is supposed to keep you safe from change, that is making all these excuses. It is your fear speaking. It is your ego speaking. It is protecting you from possible failure and disappointment.

Instead, ask yourself, "When is the right time?" Be honest! Will it ever be? What if after you have that baby you have to relocate to another country? What if the baby never sleeps and you can't work? What if you become pregnant again straight away? What if…?

I am telling you: the time is never right. If something has been on your mind for a long time and the desire is big enough, you can make it happen anyway. Don't wait any longer.

JUST DO IT – START SOMEWHERE

Just do it – without overthinking it – taking one step at a time in the right direction: that is my motto. And having interviewed numerous women for our Mums in Biz podcast about their journey, I know it works. For none of my interviewees was it the right time or an easy decision to start their own business. There were many reasons why they should not have done it. Often it was because they had little babies at home and no help. And starting your own business is not easy; it is hard work that often pays off only after many years. One thing these ladies all have in common is that they started and then took it from there. They may have had a huge goal, or they may just have had an idea or dream. But they all started and took one step at a time. They made mistakes, learned from them and tried again, and at some stage along their journey they had their first victory, which kept them going.

One of my interviews on our Mums in Biz podcast really brought home this belief for me. I interviewed Farida from Thrive Events here in Dubai. She had started her business and held her first event when she was heavily pregnant with her third child. She had no experience in events planning, but she had a dream of establishing something similar to TED Talks in Dubai. So, she started. It was bad timing, but she did not wait. That first event was a total flop; only three people showed up and she had three speakers and a photographer there. So many would have been discouraged after that, but not Farida. She learned many lessons from her first event and tried again. Her next event, which she hosted with a belly so big that I thought she might give birth right then and there was nothing like her first one – the venue was too small to hold all the people who arrived. She went on to have her baby and organised the third event. Her husband joined her, carrying their tiny baby and filming her. She breastfed in between hosting and chatting to people. This was an even bigger and better event. She has since done so many events and masterclasses and is constantly growing her business. The point of this story is that she started, just started. She gave it a try and then she did it again, without letting the circumstances or fear hold her back.

Just do it and start somewhere. What do you have to lose?

Other people's opinions? Other people seeing you fail? As I said before, most of *the other people* won't even notice. They only think about themselves. And your real friends will cheer you on and support you regardless.

I was very scared of making videos for my business for social media. What if I looked stupid? Or said the wrong thing? What about my accent when I speak English? What would people think?

What would my friends think? I know, it is super uncomfortable seeing yourself on camera. I was focusing only on the negative, seeing all the mistakes I was making, seeing all the imperfections in my skin and hair, and in my English, while also doubting my content. However, I told myself, "Done is better than perfect." So I tried, and I tried again and again. And guess what, I became better at it. I'm still not perfect. But who is? You can always find 'mistakes'. But I resonated with some people. One of my friends told me what I was doing was great, and then strangers started to comment. Now I am not scared of the camera anymore and I have motivated others to follow along and start their videos for social media.

The clue is to never overthink it and start somewhere. You need to give it a try, at least. When you realise it's for you and not actually that hard, you improve on what you have done. This does not have to be the video thing. Maybe that is not important to you (or your business, as it was in my case). Once you start, it is a huge step; every time you do it again, it is easier. You can take small baby steps. In the case of starting videos for social media, you can start by doing one video a month, then upgrading it to every two weeks and then further decrease the time between the videos. Then you can do more research and get better equipment. Because if that was the reason why you didn't start – you guessed it, it was an excuse. All you need is a phone and yourself, and of course a social media account.

ONCE I...

Something I must address in this chapter is that I was not always that way. My fear held me back so much for a long time. My go-to thoughts were, "Once I...," or "Once I am older I will be more confident," or "When I have more money and more time I will help a non-profit organisation," or "Once my mum treats me as she treats my sister, I will be happy," or "Once my dad treats me like an adult, I will happier," or "Once I have bigger boobs, I will be confident,", or "Once I have a boyfriend, I will be happy."

And of course, I made similar proclamations about material things, for example, "Once I am able to buy my own TV, it will make me happier," or "Once I move to my own place, I will be happier."

Yes, all of these things made me happier and maybe even more confident. But only for a while. This feeling could last for as little as an hour like when you buy yourself a nice new dress and are happy about it right then and there; or it could last for much longer, like the great feeling of falling in love and the beginning of a relationship, when one is on cloud nine. But the feelings never lasted forever.

I know you know this already, but it needs to be said: true happiness comes from within. And true confidence comes from within.

If you really want to do something, there is always a way. I have read numerous stories of people without money achieving incredible things, simply by believing that they could. I'm sure you have too. It often seems as though they are different. But actually, they are not; they are human beings, just like you and me.

Just recently I heard about an actress called AnnaLynne McCord, who grew up very poor in a trailer park in America. She always wanted to get away and become an actress; people laughed at her dream and said she would never make it. She proved them all wrong and made it to Hollywood and became famous. She thought once she had achieved her dream, she would be happy. However, her traumatic upbringing had not left her, so even though she had achieved what she wanted, she could not be happy. On the outside, she was living the American dream, and on the inside, she was dying. Until she found help to deal with her trauma, until she found a way to be happy from within. You can read her story on the internet; it is a great example for this chapter.

Things will not make you truly happy. A job won't make you truly happy. Money alone won't make you truly happy. The approval of your parents or a partner won't make you happy or confident. A thin body or a curvy body won't change how you feel within. Once you have all these things, your life may have changed on the outside, but it does not change on the inside.

Having a boyfriend or a husband did not make me more confident. A bigger house or a new phone, new clothes or anything like that never gave me happiness on the inside. What made me happier was how I chose to see the world, how I chose to behave, how I chose to react. The world around me did not change, the circumstances did not change, time did not change anything. I changed.

It also does not depend on anybody else's behaviour. Someone else cannot make you happy or upset. It is you who lets that happen. There is no, "Once this person doesn't do this to me anymore, I will be happier." It can help, but in the end it's up to you.

As I said before, I was easily being influenced by other people. This was true for actions and also for how I reacted to a certain people's behaviour. I would easily get very annoyed and in a bad mood. It did not affect anybody else. The other person was still happy and content; often they did not even know about my feelings. I was the only one in a bad mood; I was the one feeling stressed or unfairly treated; I was the one feeling insecure or hateful. And if someone else had similar feelings because of me or with me, and I had dragged them down, that did not help or make me feel better either. Actually, on the contrary. Once I started to feel more confident and generally happier, I began to realise that I myself could get out of these feelings a lot quicker if it was just me feeling that way.

What I learned over time is that if you are annoyed by a person's behaviour or something someone said, it is up to you. If you have a bad mood because of it or if you feel insecure, that is essentially your problem and you have to fix it. Nobody else and nothing else can fix it. People and things can help, but it is ultimately your responsibility to make sure you feel good. Other people and their actions won't make you internally happy. Things won't make you internally happy. It is your responsibility to make sure you're fine and do what you want to do; it does not happen some day because of something or someone. It is your life and your choice.

Something that people who don't know me well would never guess is that I can lose my temper easily. It may be in my character; it may be down to the way I grew up. I don't know and it is not relevant. However, I have been working on myself forever to improve that. It also comes in waves. When I was a teenager it was pretty bad. In my 20s it was much better; I was into self-development and had become a happy and confident person. I have to admit that I was challenged again (a lot) once I had kids. Being sleep-deprived, having severe morning sickness during pregnancies and the sheer exhausting work of having small kids took its toll. I am not a patient person, and my kids bore the brunt of it.

In between our move from the US to Dubai, I spent about five months with my two little sons – one was not yet two and the other one three months – alone in my home town, Hamburg. One day I saw myself and my behaviour like an angel looking in from above. I was standing in front of my two tiny humans and screaming at them in the way that my dad used to scream at me. It was something I had sworn to myself that I would never do. And here I was doing exactly that. I had the same facial expression, I had the same voice, the same body language and I guess I used the same words. I can still see myself back then, just thinking about it brings tears to my eyes and it is really hard to write about it. That was my wake-up call. Being alone and tired was not an excuse. I knew it would not truly get better once we were in Dubai and together with Gordon again or once I had more sleep or once the kids and I were less sick. I knew it was up to me to change.

And so I did. I took action. I got help with the kids; my mum came twice a week, so I could take my eldest to a music class on one day and my youngest to a postnatal gymnastics class on another. I got a babysitter for a few hours so I could work on my business again. I went to see a doctor who helped me with the stomach cramps I had, and since then I have lived lactose-free. I bought furniture and other things that made it easier for me to live with the kids in an apartment that was not mine. I accepted the situation and stopped waiting to move to Dubai to join Gordon. And I started living in Hamburg as if this was our home.

It was up to me to make the situation better. And it is still up to me. I am working on myself, on my temper and on becoming a better person every single day. I have tried so many different things and I have found many solutions that work for me and my family. For us, the most important is that I am calm and at peace with myself and within.

I HAVE LEARNED THAT I HAVE THE CHOICE TO TAKE ACTION:

1. Waiting for something, someday or someone is not going to bring me confidence or happiness. It is up to me.

2. There is never the perfect time; if I want to do something, I have to do it now.

3. I start before I am ready.

4. I just have to start somewhere.

5. I know I can always find a solution to be able to do what I want to do.

CHAPTER NINE

START, PRACTISE AND GET BETTER

So far, I have completed three half-marathons and three Half Ironman triathlons. For a long, long time, doing something like that seemed to be something for other people, not for me. Riding a road bike was for professionals like Tour de France bikers. It didn't even cross my mind that I would be able to do that. In my mind, it was the same for swimming.

You simply don't know what you can achieve until you have tried, practised and improved.

Many years ago a really good friend of mine, who was not sporty at all, suddenly decided to sign up and run the Hamburg marathon. I couldn't fathom how he would be able to do that; although I ran for fun and for staying fit, something like running a marathon had never crossed my mind. That was for other people, for fit people, who were runners. I was so wrong. He started training slowly, then he increased his run times every week and when the day of the marathon came, he was ready. I don't remember his actual time, but I do remember that he was not slow. He had achieved his dream by consistently working on it and becoming better.

I often remembered his story. He definitely inspired me, and I knew that if he could do something like that, it must be possible for me too.

In the beginning, many things sound unachievable. I have come to the conclusion however that most of the things we think are not for us, are similar to running a marathon or doing a Half Ironman. You don't wake up one morning and decide, "Today is the day I will run a marathon."

It all starts with an idea and then a dream or a vision. Then you add action, perseverance, patience and time. And one day it's part of your life; it has become a habit and eventually, your dream comes true.

THE DREAM

As a child, I had kind of given up on the thought of becoming really good at anything physical. There were always kids, and then adults, who were a lot better than I. As a teenager and young adult, I became quite good at playing golf; I realised that it was a mental game, and that I was quite suited to that. It was a game I played against myself, but for a long time being physically active was just a form of staying fit and healthy.

While living in Dubai, we have met many people who do triathlons or other types of endurance sports. I am not sure whether it's a worldwide movement, or whether it's so popular in Dubai because the weather is mostly good, or whether I simply became more aware of it. (Just when you are pregnant and suddenly the whole world seems to be pregnant too; you see only pregnant women.)

Gordon and I have always been active together. We met through sport, and that is our thing to do together, like a sports date. We used to go to the gym and to group classes; we went running and did spinning classes. But we never considered doing anything like our friends did. The more we heard about it though, the more curious we became. The stories of how other people had started, how they had gone from regularly drinking in the pub to running marathons, inspired us. It did not seem so out of our league anymore. Other people had started out being overweight and totally unfit and became these incredible athletes. It became clear to us that it was possible for us too. We just had to start somewhere.

One evening, we met another couple at a party, and they told us about a duathlon happening the following weekend. They said even their son was doing it and we should just sign up, "It's not hard – 3km run, 20km bike and another 3km run." It sounded manageable. We signed up and went and, luckily, did not think too much about it. I did this race with my normal school-run bike. Had I known that everyone else there would have a road bike and how professional the whole race would be, I would not have gone – I am sure about that. However, I did not come last, and during the run I was not the slowest. It was a good start.

This race kicked off the idea that we could get better. It took some time, but eventually we bought our first road bikes and started going on bike rides every weekend. We went very early in the morning, before the kids woke up. I started running a lot more and eventually I did my first 10km race.

A triathlon still seemed very far off, and I just couldn't swim. Well, that's not entirely true. Yes, I was able to swim without drowning, but only breaststroke with my head up. I liked it, especially during my pregnancies; it was easy on the body. However, I swam in a pool, not in the sea or a lake. I was petrified of the sea and the fish or any other sea creatures I may encounter. And I definitely did not know how to swim freestyle, or how to breathe properly without drowning, let alone how to swim fast. I honestly could not comprehend how I would be able to swim further out than a few metres from the shoreline.

My friend Akemi told me about races with very short swims. I dismissed the idea; however, the seed was planted. Eventually she showed me how to do front crawl; she even took me swimming in the sea with a group of girls once a week. I remember the first time I went, I could hardly hold the steering wheel when I drove home. And although I was slow and I panicked often, I got better and better. Over time, I lost the fear of the sea, never completely, but I now know how to handle my fear and I don't panic anymore.

One day, Gordon and I did our first sprint triathlon (sprint means 750m swim, 21km bike, 5km run) together. It was amazing. I was so proud; I had overcome my fear and had been able to do something that I thought was for other people. While doing a Half Ironman was not on my list, many triathlon races followed, and we trained more and more.

I clearly remember the summer in Germany after I had given birth to my youngest. One day, we went for a walk and we ended up by a road where thousands of runners came past doing the Hamburg half marathon, which is 21km. Suddenly I said to Gordon, "I want to do this next year." Although I had just given birth, I knew my body was a lot stronger and fitter than it had previously been. Suddenly these longer races did not seem so out of my league anymore. At that point, the longest run I had ever done was 12km, but this time I knew I could do it; I could train for it. At the end of the day, I would be running only against my mind, not against anybody else. And so I did.

I knew that if I were able to do that, I would be able to push myself further and add the swim and the bike. I had realised that like golf, triathlon and so many other sports, it's your mind and the belief that you can do it that play a major role.

I knew that if I were able to do that, I would be able to push myself further and add the swim and the bike. I had come to realise that just as with golf, the triathlon and so many other sports, your mind and the belief that you can do it play a major role.

So I trained, six days a week, sometimes twice a day. I swam, I ran and I cycled, two or three times a week, as much as my time would allow, plus I did strength training. Training for a Half Ironman is intense, especially when you have kids and a job. Every night after the kids were in bed, I started training. Sometimes I would train in the early morning. Gordon was doing it with me and we had to take turns training so that one of us was with the kids. When you read about it, it sounds impossible, but once you set a goal, once you start and are in the middle of it, it becomes normal. You just do it without thinking. What helped to keep me going was visualising and even feeling what it was like to run across that finish line.

In February 2018, I completed my first Half Ironman (1.9km swim, 90km bike, 21km run). And it was one of the most amazing feelings. No wonder running down the finish line is addictive. Nothing beats the feeling of completing the first one. I had done something neither I nor my friends and family had thought I was capable of − until I tried and did it.

That's how it happens. You start something, you practise and get better at it, and you become more confident. Suddenly new doors and dreams open and opportunities emerge.

THE START

Start – and new doors will open.

When I took a job in London many years ago, I knew I would have to fly to Hamburg every week to present our numbers in a meeting at the company's headquarters. My dream to work in another country and to progress inside the company was huge; the job sounded exciting and I knew I would learn a lot from these presentations every week. That was why I applied.

However, I was not ready. Apart from not knowing the job, there were two issues: first, I was scared of flying; and second, I was not confident about presenting. I just knew that I could learn both and I wanted to learn both.

Let's break this down. As I wrote earlier, it all starts with an idea, a dream or a thought. Then you need to start and act. If you're not starting something, ask yourself, "Why not? Is the reason valid or is it an excuse?"

Think about your bucket list, of all the things you want to do in your life. Take just one of those things and start working towards it.

If you are not starting, ask yourself whether the dream or vision you have is strong enough. Maybe it is not something you really want to achieve? My friend Barbara, whom I have known for a long time, has always been overweight. She has tried many different diets and stopped almost all of them. She kept on saying that once this or that happened, she would start again. Until one day she realised that her desire to lose weight was not that strong, not strong enough to make her persevere. She was not that unhappy and would just accept her body the way it was. Since then, she hasn't tried any more diets. She knows she is overweight, but she does not fight against it anymore. That does not mean she is putting on weight; it means she is happy with herself.

I have another friend, Kathy, who has tried many different diets, none of which ever really worked. There were many excuses and she failed many times. Eventually, she gave up and told herself, "This is now the way it is." It didn't feel right and she was still not happy. She knew deep down there was a way and needed to find the right one. The one that worked for her.

Don't give up. If your dream is big enough, it will happen. It always needs action, often failure, and a lot of consistency. Some people believe in miracles, some people believe in luck. However, both miracles and luck need action. Think of a friend who has said to you that she was not able to fall pregnant and then had a miracle baby. I'm sure that she tried many things and failed many times. However, at some point the miracle happened and she became pregnant. I have a few friends with similar experiences; they all took action first and then the miracle happened.

BECOMING BETTER

When I started the job in London, I was not good at it, but I started. I made mistakes, I learned, I failed and I learned more. I got better. Every single week. Eventually it became easier, and I became confident at presenting and flying. The experience and knowing what I was capable of back then is still with me and helps me to conquer new goals. This story may not mean as much to you as it does to me. I know many people don't care about flying or presenting. But for me it was huge. I became better and consequently more confident.

You can make any dream come true by starting, practising consistently and gaining confidence in your ability to do it. And remember it is normal not to get it right the first few times. It's OK to take time, to practise and to try again. Failing doesn't mean you have to stop. Not being good at something doesn't mean you have to stop. Continuing even if it's hard, means you will become better and it will make you more confident.

I got better at so many things I didn't think were possible. Not only presenting, flying and sport but also at being a mum, a wife and even, of course, as an entrepreneur. I got better at seemingly little things I didn't think were possible like doing my makeup or even choosing my words. And even when my improvement wasn't fast, I learned to appreciate that I did get better. I tell myself I am better than I used to be, I am better than yesterday.

To become better you have to prioritise. You have to make the time for whatever you want to achieve, and you need to make a plan. People who succeed are most often the ones who think, plan, read and look around them to find the possibilities, to notice the open doors.

Often it involves sharing one's dream and ideas. It's like our triathlon story; the more we talked about it to other people, the more we learned and the more achievable it seemed. I didn't know there were super short races you could do to start with.

The same is true for this book. I did not share this dream with anyone in the beginning. And then I started talking about it. Suddenly the dream became more real; it wasn't a dream anymore: it was a target, and a lot of new doors opened up. I learned about and met so many other authors who had published their own books, and I learned about options such as having a book coach.

With every goal you have, you need to break it up into small, achievable chunks. To achieve these chunks, you need to make the time and you have to plan ahead. Training for a Half Ironman takes a lot of time. Gordon even trained for a Full Ironman last year and it took a lot of time away from the family. When we train for a race together, we need to make sure we get our training hours in and that there is still always someone with the kids. It does require a lot of planning. Usually one of us trains early in the morning and one of us at night. It does not always work but we learn, and we adjust.

Again, the same is true for this book. I had to plan two hours each day to write. It felt a little bit like training for a marathon – a huge goal divided into chunks, which required a lot of discipline and consistency. But as the whole family was on board, everyone knew what was going on and what to expect. Even though it was during the times of the coronavirus and home quarantine, we all made it work.

By the way, having kids is a little bit like this as well. When I had no children, having children seemed like a huge step. Once I had one, the second one did not feel so out of reach anymore. Four children seemed unimaginable even to me at the time. I remember my mum telling me, "Oh yes, now you will have a gap and then you can have two more kids."

My reaction was, "Excuse me! What!" But I got better at being a mum; it became easier and after a miscarriage we suddenly both wanted a third child. By then, four kids did not seem so impossible to me anymore. I knew we would manage and figure it out. However, I have to admit, Gordon did not agree with me until he was thrown into it and had to figure it out as well, and he did very well. I am not saying having three, four or five kids or even one child is for everyone. I know there are many things to consider, especially your health, your partnership and of course finances. For example, I would happily have another child, but I know it would not work for our relationship, so I dropped that idea because I know what is more important to me.

What I want to say is that if you want something, there is a way and you will be able to manage. But you have to look at the consequences and plan well. There is always a way; remember, there is always a solution.

THE HABIT

While motivation is what gets you started, consistency is what keeps you going and growing. Things will become hard and motivation may vanish, but if you do something consistently, you don't need motivation anymore – you just do it out of habit.

A high percentage of our tasks are done on autopilot. This includes all the things we're used to, like brushing our teeth and taking a shower. Notice the things you do without even thinking about them. They're so natural to you. Driving a car is a good example. It could even be what you are thinking, the way you behave and the way you say certain things. Being on time is a habit that can be learned and unlearned. I'm quite an impatient person, which is not in my character, but just a habit of mine, and I'm working on training myself to be less impatient. We do these things without paying much attention to when and why. We just do them. They are habits.

But habits are definitely not set in stone; we can create our own new habits. You just need to do something over and over again and one day it will become the norm. Once you make the decision to achieve a goal, you find the time, start and do it regularly, and it eventually becomes a habit. Different people say different things; I have heard that a habit is formed after doing something consistently for 30 days, I have also heard 60 and 90 days. I personally feel it depends on each person as well as the task.

For me, once I have decided to do something, I'm very disciplined and can establish a habit relatively quickly. Last year, I created one new habit every month of the year. For one month I did not eat any sweets. The next month I gave up alcohol. For another month I got up at 5am every day to do yoga. Another month, I journaled every single day. Doing something for one whole month entrenched it for me quite a lot. After that month, I had taken on that habit and all the things I did, I still do at least most of the time. I do eat sweets occasionally but not much; I don't crave them anymore.

Talking about food, healthy eating is also a choice you make. Choosing what you eat every day is essentially a habit. Do you take the time to educate yourself about healthy food choices? It is not rocket science, and there is so much information out there on blogs and social media, anyone can learn about it. I don't eat as healthily as I should when I don't have much time in my day and, knowing this, I have learned new habits to make sure I do. I don't eat any ready-made meals anymore and choose fresh foods instead. Once you start thinking and enquiring about healthy eating habits, or as I did, decide not to eat certain things, it will become easier over time. Eventually, you won't miss or crave that food anymore. I was a huge cheese lover, but when I found out that I was lactose-intolerant and felt much better not eating any dairy products, I stopped eating them. That was back in 2011 and I have not missed dairy products since. It has become a habit to eat other products that I now like just as much. Again, it starts with a decision you have to make; nobody else can make that for you.

Gordon is a little different from me when it comes to habits. He often needs a goal. Last year, he set himself the goal of finishing a Full Ironman. That goal made him super focused and his daily hours-long training, combined with very good nutrition, became a habit for a year. He did not think about it much, he just did it. However, once he achieved the goal, the habit stopped as well. He took a break and only few of his routines and habits are still around.

The same is true for our thoughts. I will talk more about thoughts in the next chapter, but thinking a certain way is also a habit. For me it was a habit to think I was shy and lacking confidence. It was the normal way, the easy way, the way I was used to. It was hard to raise my hand at school. Later on, it was hard to raise my hand to volunteer doing presentations or talks or anything that had to do with public speaking. Once I had started by taking on a new job, I practised and continued every week, and it became so much easier. It eventually became a habit. Now I know, because I know my personal values and what I stand for, which voluntary tasks I will raise my hand for. If I don't raise my hand, it is not because I am not confident: it is usually because of time issues or because it is just something I am not passionate about.

Everyone is different when it comes to dreams and starting a habit. All I am doing in this book is sharing ideas and open ways of thinking, as well as showing you that it is possible. You need to find out what works for you and how you can create a habit to achieve a goal. What is important and very clear is that you need to act or think the same way over and over again, with consistency, until it becomes second nature to you, your body and your mind.

PROCRASTINATION

When you need to do something or want to adopt a new habit to achieve a goal, something that often gets in the way is procrastination. But what does it mean and why do people procrastinate?

According to Google, "Procrastination is the avoidance of doing a task that needs to be accomplished by a certain deadline. It could be further stated as a habitual or intentional delay of starting or finishing a task despite knowing it might have negative consequences."

I still remember when I learned this word in English. It was huge. And I was honestly surprised how often it was used and how much people suffer from it. Once, I was at a networking event and we were asked if we were procrastinators and almost everyone raised their hand. Which honestly surprised me. I mean, I do sometimes postpone things, but in general it is not something that I do very often, and I most certainly had not given it a word. Still, that is why I knew I had to include a part about procrastination.

The funny thing was that I did procrastinate writing this part. I think because I don't generally avoid doing things, but somehow just get on with it, I felt I couldn't say much and the fear of writing something wrong held me back. As I said, I do just get on with it. So this is my understanding of procrastination, why I believe it happens and what you can do to avoid it.

I'm sure everyone procrastinates at least sometimes. Even though I've said that I don't, if I'm honest, I do it too. There are things that I have to do, but I'm not comfortable doing them, writing an email that will upset someone or going to the dentist with my son when I know he has to have a tooth pulled. (I was so afraid for him that I postponed the appointment five times; I don't think he knew I did that.) Just like so many others I have a tendency to put off doing things that make me feel uncomfortable or that I don't like doing. My business accounting is on that list. However, and I am sure you know this, it does not get better. Just because you postpone something, doesn't mean it gets easier.

Procrastination mainly comes from a place of fear, of the unknown, of being exposed in front of other people, or because you remember an uncomfortable experience that your mind tells you to avoid it in the future. Once I realised that procrastination was fear-driven – fear of failure, fear of pain, fear of other people's opinions, essentially fear of experiencing something uncomfortable for a second time – everything made a lot more sense to me. I often wondered why people would not follow through with a diet, or why someone would not show up to exercise and yet they where successful in their jobs which requires determination. That's because they know they are good at their job, they have proven that they can do it, whereas with dieting or exercising they haven't, so instead of doing something uncomfortable, it's easier to stick to what is inside their comfort zone, something they can perform well and feel good about.

I believe that once you start, the most difficult step has been taken and it will only get easier. Once I started writing this, the words flowed out. Once I started running, it became easier every time I went. Once I sat down and looked at the numbers for my business, it felt quite satisfying because I was getting it done.

So, to avoid procrastination, you have to take action and taking action becomes much easier when you know what your end goal is. Feeling the achievement of that goal, and feeling excited about it, will make it so much easier. And honestly, if that goal doesn't excite you, then you are probably not dreaming the right dream.

Go through the chapters of this book and remember that nobody else can live your life, so nobody else can make you do things; nobody else is responsible. Remember that you can get better only by starting. Nobody is perfect and everyone started at some point. You may fail, but first, you can learn from it and try again; second, you have at least tried. You never know if you will succeed until you try. What you do know is that without action, without trying, you will not get closer to your goals.

SURROUND YOURSELF WITH LIKE-MINDED PEOPLE

When you want to achieve a goal, it is crucial to surround yourself with people who have the same or similar goals. We are motivated and we keep going when we see people working towards and achieving similar goals. Another great advantage of being around like-minded people is that they inspire you and you can learn from each other. You may find ideas that you haven't thought of or an easier or better way of doing things.

Imagine that you want to lose weight and the people you are living with don't want to or don't need to. It makes it so much harder to stay on track. But when you join a group of people who have the same goal and you connect every day, you hold each other accountable and support each other through tough days. It makes the whole process easier and even enjoyable. Achieving something alone makes it so much harder and for many people almost impossible.

When we started doing triathlons, we joined the local triathlon group. I even joined a group for a month when I stayed in Hamburg over the summer. Over time, I have met many people doing triathlons, many of whom were doing a lot more than I, and this pushed me even further. Plus, it was a lot more fun to train together. In my business life, I have a group focused on business issues and this helps me stay connected. It's a give and take situation – I learn from them and they learn from me. Like-minded people hold you accountable, push you further and essentially also make achieving a goal more fun.

So, this is how you can start today. Sit down, take out a piece of paper or your journal, write down all the things you would like to achieve. Maybe some of them are from your dream list? Pick one on that list that is your biggest dream or the most important to you right now. Or you could choose the easiest or the hardest thing on your list; it depends on how you see yourself starting. Turn to the end of the book, there is some space for you to write down two big goals. Now break that down into small achievable steps. Start creating your plan.

What do you need to do every day? When can you do it? Get your family and friends on board and share your goal. Discuss how they can support you. Maybe you can find someone who wants to join in or who can hold you accountable. Block out a time each day in your calendar or put a reminder on your phone that pops up every day. Most importantly – DO IT NOW. Not tomorrow, today. And don't forget to decide how you want to reward yourself once you have achieved the dream. Picture yourself achieving your goal. Close your eyes and see yourself achieving your goal, feel what it feels like. Whenever it gets hard, go back to that image and feeling.

I HAVE LEARNED THAT I HAVE THE CHOICE TO CREATE A HABIT, ACHIEVE A GOAL AND REALISE A DREAM:

1. To achieve something, I need to start; only by starting can I get better.

2. I need to start and ignore that inner voice of fear.

3. I need to make the time to practise and create new habits.

4. I need to visualise a successful outcome.

5. I have to share my dreams and vision for new doors to open.

CHAPTER TEN

YOUR TRUE POTENTIAL LIES OUTSIDE YOUR COMFORT ZONE

Life begins outside your comfort zone.

I saw this saying for the first time about six years ago on a cafe window in Copenhagen. The meaning was so powerful for me that it has become one of my mottos. Everything I want is just outside my comfort zone. And I have to take action, not just talk or think about it, to step outside my comfort zone and move closer to what I really want in life.

My fear of flying is still very much there. It is definitely way beyond my comfort zone. I can honestly say I would never fly, ever, but to live the life I dream of, that is not possible. My fear didn't stop me from moving abroad or moving countries; it didn't get in the way of my dream to travel.

When I was about 20, I had the chance of celebrating New Year's Eve with my family in New York. Because of my fear of flying, I didn't go. I regretted it dearly and swore to myself that this fear would not stop me from doing the things I dream of doing. The more I have flown, the better I have been able to cope and I have certainly found my ways of handling my fear. (Oh yes! A glass of wine does help during the flight, but considering the amount of time I was pregnant and breastfeeding, that has not always been an option.)

Being brave or courageous does not mean that you have no fears; it means that you are aware of your fears, but they don't stop you.

As you have learned throughout this book, I am not a natural at many things. Stepping outside my comfort zone is definitely not something that comes easily to me. It is actually something I have to force myself to do. I have many fears and I fear failure just as everybody else does. I am even afraid of my own fear. But I know that fear arises mostly because I know I will experience something unknown or I could potentially be faced with something unknown.

In my experience, if I do things that I initially thought I was not capable of, I am so much prouder of myself when I succeed. It ultimately brings me happiness. And it brings me the confidence to do more, to reach higher. Going for it and trying new things has brought me so many successes. It also brings me peace, peace within myself. I know I have tried.

Every day, I choose to step outside my comfort zone. And so can you. You will realise that when you choose discomfort, you will achieve things that you didn't think were possible.

TRYING SOMETHING NEW

Just because you haven't done it, that doesn't mean you can't do it.

My dad learned to ski when he was 19. Later on, he learned how to fly a small plane, how to sail and how to ride a motorbike. He grew up in an environment where these things and sport in general were not the norm. But once he left home, he realised that there was so much more out there. Most of us know that learning to ski when you are an adult is not easy. It is just like riding a bike or learning a new language. He did it anyway.

You can only find out what you are truly capable of by trying something new. My dad never became a great skier, but he went skiing many times and loved it. He did, however, become a great sailor and later on his lifelong dream of owning his own boat came true when he and a few friends bought one together. Some of the fondest memories of my childhood are of the great sailing holidays that we took as a family and with him. If my dad hadn't tried something he had never done before, we would never have these special memories.

Had I never tried swimming in the sea, I would not have experienced the huge victory of running over the finish line at my first Half Ironman. And ultimately giving me the knowledge that if I could achieve that in my late 30s, I can do a lot more in my life.

Personally, I am someone who maximises and achieves. Therefore, I would do only those things outside my comfort zone that bring me closer to a goal. I hardly ever do things just to prove to myself that I can do them. Everyone is different though, and some people bungee jump or skydive just to prove to themselves that it is possible.

For whatever reason you choose to push yourself out of your comfort zone, what is important is that you do it. It can be small things that you are not comfortable doing, like holding a cat or saying good morning to a stranger on the street or going to a belly dancing class, which you have secretly always been interested in but have never done. Or it can be something big, such as signing up for a marathon, jumping out of an aeroplane or travelling to another part of the world by yourself. Whatever it is for you – go back to your bucket list and see what you wrote – by doing something new, something that is slightly outside your comfort zone, you will feel a sense of pride and achievement. You will find that it is not as bad as you imagined and not nearly as difficult as you expected. You will become more confident and as this confidence grows you will keep trying new things.

By doing this, you will see so many new doors open. You will meet new people and experience things you didn't know were possible. And you will essentially grow.

FEAR

"The enemy of success is not failure. The enemy of success is fear."

This is something an amazing woman called Michelle Porter said. She speaks to my soul; it is something I tell myself every time I am scared.

Michelle Porter was a very fearful person. She decided to face her fears in the most radical way possible. For 100 consecutive days, she did one thing that scared her AND she filmed it for YouTube. She did it; she achieved things that may seem totally normal for you and me, such as driving in the dark, but were immensely scary for her. She also achieved things you may say are impossible, such as holding a tarantula. She completed her challenge successfully and has now built a business out of it, sharing her methods and teaching others how to overcome fear. She certainly achieved goals and a life she had never thought was possible. By stepping out of her comfort zone, she realised that she was capable of so much more.

Although I would not consider myself as fearful a person as she was, I do know what real, irrational fear is and that for me is of flying and falling.

My fear of flying nearly held me back from travelling on many occasions. I admit that it was often not an easy decision; my fear kept telling me not to do it. However, deep down I know I can do it. I have won so many victories over my fear, and I will not let my fear win. Having flown so many times before, even on helicopters and propeller planes, I know I am capable of doing it again. By overcoming my fears, once again, I was able to experience amazing days, make wonderful memories and definitely broaden my horizon.

The second time I gave birth was pretty horrible. My son arrived very quickly and there was no time for an epidural. Every woman is different, but pressing what felt like a football out of a tiny hole is something I remember as one of the most horrifying experiences I have ever gone through. I have to admit that I was super scared of giving birth the next time. On the one hand, I had done it before and knew it was horrible; on the other hand, I also had the comfort of knowing that it was possible. So, I did it twice more and I was fine, just like most other women giving birth, many of them just as scared as I was, or even more so.

We as humans are capable of so much more than we think. But we won't find out until we are forced to or choose to do so.

SAYING YES

For a long time, my first reaction to many things was, "No. That is not possible for me." Only after a second thought, I realised that my reaction might have been too fast, and my answer should have been, "Yes."

I remember that my dad used to say to us, "The only thing you can say is 'No, no, no'." I thought it was not true; I was saying 'no' for legitimate reasons. I realised many years later that I mostly said 'no' out of fear and because my ego was talking me out of it. My first reaction was often 'no' – I was careful, better to say 'no' than to say 'yes' and not be able to deliver.

When I became more confident, I started saying 'yes' a lot more. I pushed myself to say 'yes' before thinking about it, and then finding a way to figure it out.

There was a time when I said 'yes' too often, and because I am such a responsible person, I would overcommit.

Now I have reached the point where I know exactly what kind of things I can say 'yes' to and what kind of things I have to say 'no' to.

However, when in doubt or when my mind and ego talks to me and tells me NO, I force myself to rethink and ask myself, "Who is speaking to me right now? My fear? My ego trying to protect me from failure? Or the reality that I am taking on too much?"

One such situation, where I really have to rethink and pay attention to the voice saying 'no', is when I am asked to do a presentation or speech. This is something I love doing; it brings me great joy, but I am also still nervous every time I do it. It is outside my comfort zone, as for so many other people. And I admit I have had the opportunity to raise my hand and I wasn't quick enough. However,

I have chosen to grow and say 'yes' every time a possibility like that comes up. I have chosen to force myself to raise my hand. I don't always succeed, but I am practising and getting better at it all the time.

I heard somewhere that if you don't say 'yes' and push yourself, you will never know what is at the end of the tunnel. Meaning you will never know what you are capable of.

When I was working in London, there came a point where I knew my job was not for me anymore. I became more and more unhappy. I had chosen to stay in London with Gordon and not go back to Germany yet. During my free time, I had begun to take up evening and weekend classes at Central Saint Martins, an arts and design university. It was a step out of my comfort zone. I was surrounded by very talented people and I felt I was not a natural, but I absolutely loved it. I was surrounded by like-minded people and learned so much, not only from these classes, but also from the other students. In addition, I met amazing people, some of whom I still follow on social media and see that they have become great designers. I was thriving and I was in my happy place.

It took working with a coach to make the decision to initiate a career change into fashion design. Now that I knew my end goal, and had broken it down into pieces, I made a plan. My first step was to apply to different universities. I had to find out the process for doing that, I had to make a portfolio and, as I was a foreigner, I had to do the IELTS test, to test my English skills. I was accepted on an evening and weekend degree course, with a few girls I had met at the short courses. I had taken one step closer to my dream. I had broadened my possibilities and had said 'yes' to something new.

Unfortunately, life had other plans: Gordon got a job offer in Houston, Texas. I decided to go with him. As you can guess though,

I had totally mixed feelings. Obviously, it was a shock and felt a little bit like a punch in the face after all this work. On the other hand, I was super excited about moving to another country, which is still something I love. And to tell you the truth, it was also an easy way out of a job I did not like. Although I had made the decision to study while working, I was slightly petrified what the future might really bring. The move took it out of my hands.

I started looking into studying there, but unfortunately Houston was not exactly a design-oriented city and there were no universities offering fashion design degrees, apart from Houston community college, which offered sort of pre-degree classes, similar to the ones I had done already. I enrolled anyway. I said 'yes' to a new chapter in my life.

GROWTH

By choosing to say 'yes' and by choosing to step out of your comfort zone you will grow and you will learn. You can do this by choosing to do one small thing that you never dared to do before out of fear or discomfort. Something that will bring you closer to your desired goal or state. Once you have done it, you will be so proud of yourself and your self esteem and confidence will grow. You will learn what you can accomplish. The more you accomplish, the more these feelings of pride and achievement will fuel you to do more of what you want.

What you do is totally up to you and the step out of your comfort zone will change over time. Goals that stretched my limits a few years ago are things that I do with ease now. Trust me, there will always be something else. There will always be that next step.

Every move to a new job, a new business, to a new city, to a new country was a step outside of my comfort zone. I do things all the time that don't come easy to me but I know they are good for me and my family.

I decided I want to keep growing every day by choosing discomfort over comfort. I decided to keep on growing and becoming a better person, mother and wife by working on myself all the time. I will not allow myself to accept my behaviour; I will always choose to reach for the best behaviour. In addition, I decided I would keep on learning about human behaviour as well as my own, about personal growth and what is possible. What I share in this book is what has allowed me to achieve this best behaviour, what has worked for me so far. What I want you to take away from this book is that you always have a choice and one choice should be to say YES more. Don't overthink things: just do them.

This is the core belief that I try and pass on to my kids every single day. I often hear them say things such as, "No, I can't do this," or "No, I am not a runner", or "No, I don't dare" or "I am just not good at this," or some similar statement. They do this more and more as they get older. This is totally normal; kids become more aware of their own abilities, of their peers and surroundings. What I try to do is teach them to not limit themselves with their own negative thoughts, or worse, other people's abilities and behaviour. My strategy is to lead by example and live outside my comfort zone and be honest about it to my children. They know that I do things I don't feel comfortable doing. And by sharing that openly I hope to help them believe in themselves and I show them what they can be capable of.

I HAVE LEARNED THAT I CAN MAKE THE CHOICE TO STEP
OUTSIDE MY COMFORT ZONE TO LIVE THE LIFE I DREAM OF:

1. I don't know what is at the end of the tunnel if I don't try.

2. I constantly train my mind to make YES my first choice.

3. Just because I haven't done it before, doesn't mean I can't do it. We are all capable of so much more.

4. When I choose discomfort, I achieve things that I didn't think were possible.

5. Going outside of my comfort zone ultimately brings me confidence.

CHAPTER ELEVEN

THE TRUTH IS YOU NEED TO BELIEVE IN YOURSELF

…or nobody else will.

I used to believe that I needed other people to believe in me. Now I know I was wrong. Most importantly, I have to believe in myself; what counts is my own opinion – positive or negative – of myself. We often hear, "You need to believe in yourself." It is said so easily, but I know how hard it actually is. However, this is the most important step towards living a life full of confidence. And it all starts within yourself and what you tell yourself. The thoughts you choose.

YOU BECOME WHAT YOU TELL YOURSELF

Your thoughts, your emotions and your actions are all connected. If I keep telling myself that I can't do something, I will never be able to do it. However if I tell myself in my mind what I can achieve, if I picture myself achieving it, my emotions will change and become positive. I am so much more likely to be able to achieve what I want to achieve.

I used to play a lot of golf, which is primarily a mental game. When I told myself that I couldn't play a particular shot, I would fail. If I imagined how I would hit the ball, how it would fly and where exactly it would land, I increased my chances of doing exactly that by a very high percentage. I can clearly remember a game of golf where I played against another player in a match play. The rules of match play mean that the person with the fewest number of shots for that hole wins. Whoever wins the most holes wins the match. On this particular day, it looked as though I was losing; I can't remember how many holes I was down, but it was quite a lot. Then I hit a bad shot and had to play over many trees to even reach the green. It looked like another lost hole. But something shifted in my mind. I just knew I would hit that ball on to the green and close to the flag. And I did. To everyone's surprise, I won that hole. From that moment on I knew I could turn this match around. Everything started to work; I could clearly picture every shot in my head, no matter how difficult they were, and my actions followed. I started winning hole after hole. In the end, I won a match that had seemed like a lost cause because I had told myself that I will win.

Experience tells me that this works in reverse as well. Once one bad shot is played, many others follow because you don't believe in yourself anymore. You can't turn the game around, because you can't turn your thoughts around. The greatest athletes are those who can win this battle of negative thoughts in their mind and turn a match around; they never give up. There are a lot of studies around sport and how athletes can become better at and influence their game just by playing it in their mind.

If this is true for sport, I feel it is true for life too. You can rehearse your actions and your life in your head. And depending on what you concentrate on, it will become reality. So choose your focus wisely.

Unfortunately, people – especially women – are often super hard on themselves. We criticise ourselves constantly. We tell ourselves things that we would never say out loud to other people and I am sure we would never dare say them out loud to ourselves.

I have done exactly that. I had thoughts such as "I am shy", "I can't do this", "I can't just go and talk to that stranger", "I will never earn enough money." I have looked in the mirror and told myself "I am not pretty enough". My guess is you know what I am talking about. Until I realised what I was doing, how I was influencing myself in a destructive way. So, I decided to actively choose what I am thinking about myself. I learned to change my thoughts around into something positive. These days I still have destructive thoughts, sometimes; the difference is that now I realise when I do this, and I know what to do to stop myself and turn the thoughts around.

What I want to say is that it is normal to have negative thoughts sometimes. I have them too – it is human. However, do not let them take over your life. It is important that you can recognise them. Ask yourself whether you would say what you just told yourself to anybody else. Or what you would feel if someone else told you that. And ask yourself whether this is really the truth or are you telling yourself something to protect yourself from disappointment, fear of failure or fear of the unknown.

Although I have had destructive thoughts, there are a few things in my life that I have been totally certain about since I was little. Some of them I had forgotten myself. My childhood nanny told me that I always used to say I would live in a hot and sunny country. And it is true – although I was thinking I would live in Spain, which was at the time the only hot country I knew, I now live in Dubai and it can't get much hotter. I can't explain it but somehow, I just always knew I would live abroad.

Often people ask me how I managed to have two boys first and then two girls. Although I admit that I did try to manipulate the sex of our next baby after having two boys through the timing of conception (which did not turn out the way I had planned it), I did not really believe in all that. Deep down I just knew, I knew I would have a girl. Deep down I knew I would have two boys and two girls. I was so certain about it. It is a feeling I can't explain, but whenever I really want to achieve something, I work on repeating this feeling of absolute certainty.

CHANGE YOUR THOUGHTS, CHANGE YOUR LIFE

"Whether you think you can, or you think you can't – you're right."

Henry Ford

If I tell myself I am not a swimmer, I can feel the fear of swimming in the sea build up inside me and I don't go swimming. Our brains can't distinguish between what is reality and what is not. In other words, my brain does not know whether I am physically able to swim or not, or whether I am just thinking I can't swim. So, the first step I need to take is to manipulate my thoughts and to make myself believe I am a swimmer. Because I feel confident in my swimming abilities, I will be a lot less scared of the sea and I will give swimming in the sea a try. I then choose to do it again. I practise, I become better at it and my thoughts change automatically to be more positive because I feel confident in my abilities. Over time, I naturally think I am a swimmer. In addition, I will be less scared of the sea and I may even love swimming. Initially, swimming was a huge step out of my comfort zone, but by changing my thought pattern, I became more confident and swimming in the sea is no longer a big step – the fear can even vanish.

I heard somewhere on a podcast, that the same is true when you think you have to do something. By telling yourself you 'have to', you are essentially taking away your choice. I hope that by now you know you have choices. You know that you don't need to think, "I have to". You never 'have to' do anything. You can choose to. Or you can say, "No, thank you."

As you can see, you can choose your thoughts. You can choose what you believe about yourself. You can choose your own perception of yourself. Because everything is how you yourself perceive it and you can always choose to perceive things, people and yourself, a different way.

Start by telling yourself who you are. By telling yourself that you are a confident person, you are a happy person, you are a calm person, you are a strong person. And so on.

You can do this by writing it down in your journal every day, or you can look in the mirror and repeat the words out loud or you can sit and meditate. These are a few of the ways that I use every day. I meditate every morning and I have a mantra that plays in my head, "I am calm and relaxed, I am calm and relaxed, I am calm and relaxed." Because I tell myself that early in the morning, before my day starts, I can handle everything that comes my way – often the children – a lot calmer and more relaxed.

Thoughts are so powerful; they can change your life. When there is something in your life that you are not happy about, the first step is often to change your thoughts. Your emotions and then actions will follow automatically. When I am going to give a speech, I visualise myself doing it many times before the actual speech. I can see the room, I can see the people and I can even feel the event. I can feel the positive feelings and my doing well. I have done the same many times during my training for the Ironman. This time not during a meditation, but while I was actually training. I could see myself and feel my emotions running down that finish line. I knew I would not fail; I knew I would finish.

You can do the same with your family. Picture yourself behaving the way you want to behave when interacting with your family and your kids. See yourself from the outside, listen to the words you are using, feel what it is like to act that way. And tell yourself in your head or even write it down, for example, "I am a calm mum," or "I am a good listener," or "I am a good supporter." Whatever it is you want to work on, it starts in your mind.

Obviously, this is so much harder when you have other people in your life who keep telling you who you are. If you are being told all the time that you are lazy and never help other people, it is much easier to just give in to that and follow what you are being told. It is much harder to work against that and tell yourself that you are hard-working and helpful. However, I am telling you, it does work. I have done exactly that. And I still do it.

CHANGING THOUGHTS AND PERCEPTION

As I mentioned in Chapter 4, perception is the way you look at something through your eyes with yourself in mind.

When I was writing this part, it was my son Nicholas's ninth birthday. For you, this was just any other day. For Nicholas, it was a day he had been looking forward to for weeks, even months. He was waiting to be the centre of attention and of course for his presents. For his siblings, it was exciting because it was a different day in our house, and they got to party with him. For me, the birthday of any of my kids carries a few different feelings, thoughts and meanings. One of them is that I love seeing my child so happy and excited; the whole day his or her eyes sparkle with joy.

However, a birthday also means more work. I have to organise presents, a party, a cake and so on. And to be honest, I am often glad when it's over. But most importantly, it is also always a day full of memories of the past years and my child's actual birth, so I am filled with joy and gratitude. We all look at my son's birthday, and any other event, with a totally different perspective and it is usually determined by our own experiences around that or a similar situation.

This year, 2020, Nicholas's birthday was somehow a very emotional day for me and a good example of changing thoughts and perception. I couldn't believe Nicholas was already nine years old; I remember the day he came rushing into this world as though it were yesterday, even though so much has happened since then. I remember clearly how Maximilian, only 17 months old, walked hesitantly into the hospital room, peeking around the corner, curious to see what had happened. We spent the rest of the day with my parents in the hospital watching the Masters (a big golf tournament). It was also the five years to the day since Gordon and I had started dating.

Because of Covid-19, this year's birthday was celebrated in complete lockdown in Dubai and we were not even allowed to invite any friends over for a party. We spoke to our family and friends back home via Zoom (not a new thing, but somehow it was so different because of lockdown). I can't explain why, but I was not as happy as I expected to be. There was this strange feeling of disbelief and maybe I even felt a little depressed.

Seeing my son so happy, made me happy, but I felt this hollow sensation that I could not name. My son didn't care; it was his birthday and he got to be the centre of attention, he could choose his favourite meal, he got to be with us and of course he was happy about his presents.

I had to step out to go to the supermarket; I needed a permit to go, and I had to wear a mask and gloves. At the supermarket, you had to wait outside because they only allowed a few people in at a time. We had to queue up outside with the measured distance between us. When it was my turn to go in, I had to have my temperature taken. It was a surreal experience. I cycled back home and realised that the streets were totally empty. At the end of our road, a little girl was playing alone in front of her garage. It felt as though I had stepped into a film scene. I was overwhelmed by feelings and had tears in my eyes. My thoughts started to become negative, "What if this goes on forever? What will happen after this? Will we ever be able to hug our friends again? When will we be able to visit my parents again? When will the kids be able to play with their friends again? What about all the women giving birth right now? Some without their husbands, but all definitely without their parents."

By the time I got back home, my thoughts were in a negative spiral and I could feel a depressed mood settling over me. I took a deep breath and got my thoughts in order. This was not who I wanted to be, this is not who I am, and it was certainly not the person I wanted to be for my son on his birthday. So, I acknowledged my feelings, but then changed my thought pattern; I changed my perspective. I started telling myself positive stories instead of negative scenarios.

I told myself that I would go to Germany in the summer and spend time with my parents, even if it was only in their garden a few metres away. I thought about the idea of a big joint birthday party where all my kids could celebrate together at the end of the year. I thought about small things, such as waking up a little later tomorrow morning because it was the weekend. I told myself to think about the things I wanted to do with the kids over the weekend and the things I wanted to do for myself. I made myself look at all the positive things we were experiencing right now. I found something to laugh about with Gordon, I hugged my kids and we all watched *Harry Potter* together. I had managed to shift my thoughts (and my mood) and look at the day from a different perspective. It felt much better, I enjoyed the rest of the evening with the whole family and we had a great time together.

What I want to say with this story is that when you catch yourself thinking negative thoughts about a situation, about yourself or someone else, try to reverse the thoughts and think exactly the opposite. In my case, instead of concentrating on all the negatives, I made myself look at the positives right in front of me. Those were the things that really mattered in that moment. I could not control the situation outside, but I could control my thoughts. Try that the next time when you are feeling down or depressed. And when your thoughts are more general like being a shy person you can, instead of thinking, "I am shy," say to yourself, "I am in the process of becoming confident." Or instead of, "I am fat," say to yourself, "I have a beautiful female body."

Another idea may be when you are thinking that you are nervous to flip that thought into, "I am excited." I often tell myself that nerves are good, it means my body is alert and I will perform better. When you come across a difficult situation or task and you feel overwhelmed, instead of saying, "I can't," say to yourself, "I will give it a try," or instead of thinking of it as 'a problem', think to yourself, "This is a challenge, but I will find a way." By doing that, you give yourself a choice and it will code your brain into looking for possibilities.

If you are not happy with something, a situation, choose to change your perception. Change the way you look at the situation and it will look different to you. If you are upset with someone or you don't understand the behaviour of a person, make yourself look at them from someone else's perspective and the way you perceive the behaviour of the other person will change. You cannot change people and you cannot change a situation, but you can change the way you look at it; you can change your thoughts about it; and you can change the way you react to it. In this way, you can help yourself. It will make you happier. A person or a situation cannot upset you or annoy you; they can only upset or annoy you if you allow them to.

BE CONTAGIOUS WITH YOUR BELIEFS

Earlier I spoke about how you become who you surround yourself with. This works the other way too. If you are behaving and believing a certain way, you can become infectious to others. Others will start behaving and seeing the world the way you see it.

Once you choose to tell yourself positive things, once you choose to believe in yourself, once you shift your mind, your thoughts shift to the positive and you begin to feel, act and look like your chosen way. The people who surround you will follow your actions; they will believe in you. This is so easy to see with our kids. If parents, or even older siblings, feel frightened and show or talk about their fear in a certain situation, their kids, or younger siblings, will adopt that feeling and may have similar fears. For example, my friend Sarah, who was scared of walking across the shutters that lie over the drainage systems and although she didn't say that, her son saw how she avoided them, so he also started walking around them. Or my daughter Felicia is petrified of cats, her younger sister Lavinia sees that every day and has for no reason adapted that fear. She has learned it from her older sister.

And of course it works the other way around. I choose to be happy and joyful every day; some days I am more successful than others. But if one of us in the house is joyful and happy, it is contagious: I can see how the rest of the family starts to feel the same way.

You need to believe in yourself for others to believe in you. As a business owner, I have to constantly sell myself. If I don't really believe in myself, in my potential, my customers will feel that straight away. They will notice this by the subtle words I use and by my body language. If I say things like "I think" or "It could be", it doesn't sound very convincing. If I don't believe in my abilities or my product, I will automatically use the words that show that. And this is true for life; we show our true feelings through behaviour, the words we use and the way we say things. Behaving in a way that is not actually you, will reveal itself at some point.

If you think of a really good salesperson you may notice that they look and sound very sure of what they are selling. They often speak loudly and are somehow captivating with their mood. They are so sure of themselves and their product that they make others feel the same way. Basically, that is what you want to achieve about yourself. Believe so strongly in yourself and your abilities that others will do so too.

THINGS THAT HAVE HELPED ME

A few years ago, I started writing everything I want to achieve as if it had already happened. For example, for this book I wrote that I was a published author. I meditate almost every morning and tell myself positive affirmations as well as picture myself doing the things I want to accomplish. I write down lots of notes with quotes I like or positive reminders. I used to have them above my computer in my office, so I would see them every day. Even if I didn't look at them consciously all the time, I would still read them from time to time and be reminded. I also have a poster with all the words describing how I want to present myself in the world inside my cupboard. Whenever I open my wardrobe, I read them. And in addition, my kids read them too. These notes not only hold me accountable, but the kids read them, and I am sure something is sinking in and will stick with them for their future.

I started writing on the mirrors in our house. These can be quotes or just something I want to say to myself or my kids. The kids love that too; not only are they allowed to write on a mirror, but they have become experts in making up great sentences of their own and writing them as reminders on their own bathroom mirror or for me on mine. One example of something my son wrote on my mirror and that is still on there is, "The best way to predict your future is to create it." He had found this in his school on a wall and now keeps reminding all of us. This is a playful way of influencing our minds in a positive way.

I once read somewhere in a book that you should write down, "I love you," on your bathroom mirror and tell yourself every morning either out loud or in your head, "I love you." Even if you don't say it out loud, you will see it every time you look in the mirror. I felt a bit strange at first – talking to myself in the bathroom telling myself, "I love you," but the power of these words makes such a difference. It works, go on give it a try.

A vision board can be another powerful tool and I have created vision boards for myself and with my kids. In short, we cut out images from magazines that represent our dreams and goals and we stick them on a big board. This can be something we want to have, achieve or be. Just as a reminder every single day. Sometimes we include some powerful words as well. I usually keep my vision board in my bedroom or my office, and the kids stick them on their walls. Not only do they look nice and creative, but because we see them and are reminded every day, our subconscious mind starts working towards our dreams and goals. For me, it is a great reminder of why I do what I do.

We build ourselves up by standing in front of the mirror and repeating the things we can do – this is my daughter's favourite exercise. When she was afraid of speaking in front of the class, we kept standing there, holding hands and she kept saying to herself, that she is strong and can speak in front of the class with ease. We tell ourselves that we are strong, we are beautiful, we are intelligent and a few other positive affirmations almost every day. Even when Lavinia was only three years old, she was already an expert at this and loved it; even if it was more of a game for her.

I also send myself reminders on my phone about how I want to feel and show up today. Every single day. This is something I have picked up from Brendon Burchard, who has many great ideas on creating habits.

As you may have guessed, I am constantly exploring spiritual and self-development. I'm completely open to trying out new ideas or ways to empower myself and grow. Tell me something that has worked for you in certain situations and I will see if it works for me. Over the years, I have tried many new habits. I have explored mantras, quotes on my phone, mediation, yoga, journaling, self-development conferences, books, you name it. Some people have resonated with me, some not so much. Some things have worked, some haven't. What works for me doesn't need to work for you and vice versa. What you need to do is find the things that work for YOU. But you can do that only by trying. Try to stand alone in your bathroom all naked and tell yourself, "I love you." I know the thought of it is so weird. However, you never know, maybe that is all you need at that moment and it will change how you think and feel in no time. But you need to choose to start.

CONFIDENCE

One of my favourite sayings on my wall is one that Kyla gave me, "She believed she could, so she did." If something seems impossible, even for a long time, once you make the choice to believe in it, it is already happening, you are making it happen. The only impossibilities are the ones you create in your head. Things may look as though they are impossible. But if you believe in making it happen, you can. It starts with a belief, a goal and then just starting.

Doing a Half Ironman seemed totally impossible for me for most of my life and now I can only say to you: don't limit yourself by what things look like to you in a certain moment or situation. Don't limit yourself because of what others say to you or what you think they may think. Don't limit yourself by what has happened in the past. Believe you can and then go and do it.

My belief about confidence used to be that you had to be outspoken, loud, look different and always know the answer – basically, if you were confident, you were the perfect person. And while I learned that this was not true by observing people, I also learned it by changing and becoming confident. I am still not a loud or outspoken person and I don't look any different and most importantly I am not perfect. I am confident because I changed my beliefs. I am now calm inside. I love myself. I have values for my life that I live by. I don't listen to other people. I am not letting my past define me. I have tried things and failed, and I have tried things I thought I would never be capable of and succeeded. I have surprised myself. I am confident because I look for and believe in the positives in life and in people. I am confident because I am happy. And that is what I want to pass on to you.

There is always a way, there is always a solution. You just have to choose to look for it. Choose to listen to yourself and believe in yourself. Choose to be positive, choose to be joyful, choose to give. And finally choose to be confident, choose to be the person you were born to be. Choose to live YOUR life.

I HAVE LEARNED THAT I CAN MAKE THE CHOICE WHAT I BELIEVE ABOUT MYSELF:

1. I become what I tell myself.

2. Once I believe I can do it, I will do it.

3. I am responsible for the perception and beliefs of how I view my own life, myself and other people.

4. The only impossibilities are the ones I create.

5. Confidence is a choice.

KEEP ON DREAMING

While I was writing this book, there was one thought that never left me, one essential life lesson I want to pass on to you and to my children, Maximilian, Nicholas, Felicia and Lavinia.

Keep on dreaming!

I don't mean daydreaming. I mean imagining your dream life.

And then don't ever give up on that dream!

Whatever you do with your life, don't ever let anybody talk you out of your dream. Not you yourself, not anybody else and not the circumstances. Your dream is much bigger than that.

A job that you don't like but pays well will never make you as happy as a job that you love and are passionate about but doesn't pay as well. A seemingly perfect person or condition will never make you as happy as those that you love and are passionate about. Your dream is more important.

Dreams may change and that's OK, but never give up dreaming. Remember often the theme of your dream stays the same. All I can say is listen to it. Working on that dream will make you happy.

Besides living with my husband in a hot country, having a big family, traveling the world and giving back to the children who are not as fortunate, I wanted to be a fashion designer. I am still working on that last dream.

If you ever had a childhood dream and it hasn't changed much but you haven't done it, now is the time to start. Do not let the chance slip by, do not look back at your life one day, thinking I should have…

Make the choice to follow your dream.

With much love

xx Emilia

ABOUT THE AUTHOR

Emilia Ohrtmann is a multi-passionate entrepreneur, blogger and co-host of the Mums in Biz Podcast. As a website designer and consultant, she helps female entrepreneurs start their dream businesses. She is a certified neurolinguistic programming (NLP) coach and always on the lookout for new opportunities.

Emilia left the corporate world in 2007 when she moved with her husband to Houston, Texas and started her first design business. Since then, she has reinvented herself constantly. It is Emilia's passion to support women to become confident and to be their true selves.

She hails from Germany, has lived in four different countries and with her husband and their four children she currently calls Dubai their home.

For more information visit www.emiliaohrtmann.com or www.emiliasjourney.com.

MY DREAM LIST

THINGS I AM GRATEFUL FOR

....

....

....

....

....

....

....

....

....

....

....

....

GOALS I WANT TO ACHIEVE

Goal number 1:

....

Step 1:

....

Step 2:

....

Step 3:

....

Step 4:

....

Step 5:

....

Goal number 2:

....

Step 1:

....

Step 2:

....

Step 3:

....

Step 4:

....

Step 5:

....